CAREER WARFARE

10 Rules for Building a Successful Personal Brand and Fighting to Keep It

David F. D'Alessandro

with Michele Owens

McGraw-Hill

New York Chicago San Francisco Lisbon London
Madrid Mexico City Milan New Delhi San Juan Seoul
Singapore Sydney Toronto

The *McGraw·Hill* Companies

1 2 3 4 5 6 7 8 9 0   AGM/AGM   0 9 8 7 6 5 4 3

ISBN 0-07-141758-3

Printed and bound by Quebecor World.

McGraw-Hill books are available at special quantity discounts to use as premiums and sales promotions, or for use in corporate training programs. For more information, please write to the Director of Special Sales, Professional Publishing, McGraw-Hill, Two Penn Plaza, New York, NY 10121-2298. Or contact your local bookstore.

  This book is printed on recycled, acid-free paper containing a minimum of 50% recycled, de-inked fiber.

For Michael, Andrew, and Robert

CONTENTS

ACKNOWLEDGMENTS

Years ago, I had a boss who told me the problem with successful people is that as they get older, they fancy themselves to be philosophers—as if their success had something to do with cosmic thoughts that only *they* could have discovered.

I have never forgotten his comments.

This book is written to be anti-philosophical and, ultimately, practical. Most business books are either theoretical wastelands, pedantic drivel, or self-congratulatory tomes. In this book the real message is that you don't need complicated theories to succeed in business or in any other field—you just have to listen and watch carefully. All the signposts you need are nearby, in the people around you and in the events that unfold daily. I only offer my own observation of the good, the bad, and the ugly, the outrageous, the comedic, the desperate, and the serious to help you avoid the mistakes I made and, hopefully, find your own route to success.

This book came to pass because of many people who have helped me see the light. I would like to recognize a few: Steve Burgay, a Hancock senior vice president who encouraged me to write a more personal book than *Brand Warfare*; his advice, as always, was sterling. Becky Collet, a lawyer and Hancock PR person, who is always prodding me to new heights and catching me when I fall. Michele Owens, who is the real writer here, a marvelous scribe and a unique person for whom I have great affection. John Sasso, whose incredible insights helped me to edit this book. Mary Glenn, my McGraw-Hill editor, whose guidance and patience are remarkable.

I also want to thank my wife Jeannette for her unwavering encouragement during the inevitable ups and downs of writing this book.

I would normally thank the many lawyers who combed over every word many times. But I refuse—because, while right, they were a pain.

Most of all, I would like to thank the characters in the book. Hollywood could not have scripted them; they are all too human, too real, and so vital in helping me navigate my career.

INTRODUCTION

The real tests in business are never quite what you expect.

Let me tell you about a decisive moment in my career. I was about 30 years old, and I was making my first presentation before the board of directors of the firm I now worked for. My company had recently been absorbed by this company, so I was completely new to management—an enslaved representative of a conquered nation. Yet it was up to me to lead the discussion of what the combined organization should now be named.

I had spent *weeks* on this presentation because I'd never spoken in front of such a senior group of executives before.

It was an intimidating audience. The chairman himself was straight from Central Casting. Let's call him "Reggie." Reggie had all the CEO gestures down, including a little wave that he would give to dismiss you. People never quite walked next to him; they were always a step behind.

And he never went anywhere without a group of malevolent-looking guys in tow, who did his "wet work" for him. They sat around the conference table like a series of villains out of Dick Tracy—the CFO with a little sneer on his face, another looking as warm and friendly as a barracuda in big Coke-bottle glasses.

I took a deep breath and was about to begin, when the chairman said to me, "HRS SHYNN RRR TTD U YRRR VRRRY TTRTV YNN MNN?"

I was stumped.

I'd thought I was prepared. I knew everything, of course, except what really counted: the fact that these board meetings took place immediately following lunch, and that at lunch, wine was always generously served. So by the time the meetings got under way, Reggie was relaxed and ready for some chocolate mints. He would sit in the boardroom with a box of After Eight dinner mints in front of him.

Would he offer one to anyone else? No. He'd just put one after another on the roof of his mouth.

As the square-shaped mint melted into the contours of his mouth and then slowly, slowly dripped into the back of his throat, the rest of the room would wait breathlessly for it to disappear. Because until it did, no one could understand a single word he said. In effect, he gave himself a speech impediment, and the meetings would take three times as long as they should have, because of his mints. And everyone pretended not to notice.

But I had never been to a board meeting before, so I had no idea how to proceed. "I'm sorry, sir," I said. "I didn't quite understand you."

"HRS SHYNN RRR TTD U YRRR VRRRY TTRTV YNN MNN?" he said again.

By this point, my boss and his buddies in the back of the room were struggling to stifle their laughter. But to me, this was a critical moment in my career. The chairman of the board was addressing me before I'd presented. And I didn't know what he was talking about.

"Excuse me, sir?" I said.

Now he was starting to get mad. But I caught a break. A brief window suddenly appeared when one mint had melted away and he hadn't yet popped in another.

"Has anyone ever told you," he said, practically shouting at me, "that you're a very attractive young man?"

At this, my boss and some of the guys sitting in the peanut gallery practically fell off their chairs laughing. The Dick Tracy villains at the table, on the other hand, were pros at maintaining face. They suddenly found the reports that had been sitting in front of them for the entire luncheon—and those reports suddenly became fascinating reading. Wow. Armies of numbers marching across the pages. How gripping.

As for me, I finally understood the individual words he was saying, and I was *still* sure I'd misheard him.

"Pardon me?" I said, once again.

"For the last time," he said, so fed up with me that he was turning red, "has anyone ever told you that you're a very attractive young man?"

I hesitated just a moment. I felt as if I were listening to an announcement from the Emergency Broadcast System. A siren was wailing in my head, and a voice-over said, "This is a test."

I thought, "This is a test—and not with the chairman, because he's a lunatic. This is a test with the hitmen."

Indeed, they looked as expectant as the attendees at a NASCAR event, coolly anticipating a car crash. I knew it was important for me to play to them and not say something witless. Had anyone ever told me I was attractive?

"Thank you very much," I said politely to the chairman, "but not in this kind of environment."

Reggie seemed satisfied with my answer. Its effect on everyone else, though, was to *really* separate the men from the boys. The hitmen, leafing through their reports, knew better than to laugh at their leader. The board members, many of them quite elderly, were just happy to still have somewhere to wear their suits. The boys in the peanut gallery, on the other hand, absolutely collapsed with mirth. Strangled guffaws could be heard from the back of the room.

As a presenter, I was destroyed. After the comedy that had preceded it, my presentation was completely anticlimactic, 15 or 20 minutes of white noise that was of zero interest to anyone. And at the end of the thing, the chairman said, "WTTT BTTT FDDRKR?"

Once again, no one had a clue as to his meaning. When he finally cleared his mint, we learned that he and his wife had taken a trip to South Carolina the previous weekend and had seen a place called Fuddruckers.

"You know," he said thoughtfully, "that name kind of stuck with me. Maybe we should think about buying this company called Fuddruckers and calling ourselves Fuddruckers."

Now, we were a financial services company. We'd spent tens of thousands of dollars on research and hundreds of thousands of dollars on new designs, all in an attempt to come up with a dignified identity for our business. And the chairman thought we should call ourselves Fuddruckers.

The meeting was over. By this time, I was ready to go home, sit in a warm bath, and slit my wrists. I thought this appearance in front of the board had been a career-destroying disaster. Actually, it hadn't been. My initial instincts had been right. This had been a very important test—one that I had passed.

Sure, Reggie had been bizarre. But if I had reacted badly to him, it would have been my reputation that was crushed, not his. He had way too much power. His being bizarre was an accepted mode of operation, and, eventually, they'd be able to force him out. If, I, however, had been impolite, or had appeared ruffled, or had been so rattled by him that I couldn't continue the presentation, it would have doomed my chances of rising within the organization because the others would have seen me as unable to handle an adverse circumstance.

Fortunately, I had kept my head, and for weeks afterwards, people were congratulating me on how I'd handled the chairman.

It turned out to be a tremendous shortcut for me. In the ordinary course of business, it might have taken me years even to make it onto the radar screen of this group of senior executives. But in 10 minutes, I went from being a faceless nobody to someone the henchmen knew—and knew not to trifle with. I made more powerful friends in that one peculiar moment than I would have even thought possible.

Here is the significant point: I went into that meeting thinking that it was the quality of my presentation that counted, and I came away from the experience understanding that it was how I'd handled myself that really mattered, because it gave me a reputation.

I tell this story because this is how business really works.

Most of us assume that if we follow our parents' advice—work hard, be polite, dress neatly—we will be given every opportunity to succeed. And these things are all necessary; they are the minimum daily requirements for any professional career, you might say. But by themselves, they will not set you apart from your peers, and they will not propel you into the executive suite.

> **Hard work and accomplishments are necessary. But they probably will not set you apart from your peers.**

In fact, the biggest mistake you can make is to assume that organizations are rational, and that success will proceed in a rational manner from your good performance reviews, nice manners, and sharp suits.

Organizations are *not* rational, any more than your average small town in Ohio is rational. Corporations are just vertical villages, as full of eccentricity, rashness, and pettiness as any dot on the map.

Like small towns, they have a mayor, a planning board, and a town drunk—maybe more than one.

Like small towns, they are driven by gossip, intrigue, and anecdote.

Just as no one can avoid developing a certain kind of fame in a small town, no one can avoid developing a certain kind of fame within an organization, either.

And, just as in a small town, the really juicy opportunities are usually doled out in a way that makes "competitive bidding" seem suspect. In other words, the jobs do not always go to those who look best on paper.

So what really separates those who simply plod along through their careers from those who excel? In my experience, it's the name you make for yourself on Main Street.

> **Most organizations are just vertical villages. What really counts is the name you make for yourself on Main Street.**

Everyone in organizational life is constantly being watched and evaluated by bosses, clients, vendors, peers, subordinates, and these people's significant others. Every day, with every bit of human interaction you engage in, some member of this crowd forms an opinion about you.

The professional world is a very small place, and everybody talks. Your bosses talk, your clients talk, your vendors talk, your peers talk, and your subordinates talk. And the significant others *really* talk. They talk about you whether you're a lone salesperson with your own territory or the CEO at the top of the heap. Eventually, those thousands of opinions that are created by thousands of transactions will generate a kind of consensus about who you are.

That consensus goes by many names: It is your reputation, public image, legend, or character. This is probably my bias as a marketer who has spent decades helping corporations build *their* reputations, but I like to think of it as a "personal brand." But no matter what you call it, more than anything else, that collective opinion will determine whether you conquer the vertical village or are defeated by it.

Don't believe me? Let's consider, then, how big promotions are really won. I've been in thousands of meetings in which someone's future was being decided. And it may shock you to learn that in these meetings, there is no big chart where everyone is ranked by merit.

> **More than anything else, your personal brand will determine whether you conquer the vertical village or are defeated by it.**

It may also shock you to learn that the people who are in a position to actually *do* something about your career do not think about you all the time. I guarantee that they think about you only one-tenth of one percent of the time you spend thinking about yourself.

Instead, decisions about your future are likely to be made in the most casual way, after a series of people—or even just one person—expresses an opinion about you. It's like a Rorschach test. Somebody flashes your name. What leaps to mind? Eats peanut butter and liverwurst for lunch? Or has a really unique vision for the business?

Somebody will say, "She's smart, but no one wants to work with her." Or, "He's not a genius, but he's loyal and he knows how to motivate people." Or even, "He came unglued at the board meeting last week when the chairman told him he was cute." And you will either get the opportunity you covet—or not.

If you work until you're 65, there will be maybe five or six of these brief moments that will determine how well you are rewarded for your years of effort.

> **Promotions are usually doled out in the most casual way, based on someone's instant assessment of you.**

The window of opportunity may be narrow, but what's at stake can change the course of your life forever. And an instant assessment of you in one of these moments means more to your career than a foot-high stack of performance appraisals in your personnel file. So you'd better be prepared.

Yes, you'll have to have worked hard. That's a given.

Yes, you'll have to have accomplished something tangible in order to be in the running for the job, the partnership, or the venture capital at all. Organizations respect measurable results. But it's *how* you get those results that gets you to the next level.

The deciding factors, more often than not, are qualities that are not measurable but that are just as important to an organization as the numbers. I'm talking about personal qualities, such as honesty, or focus, or fearlessness, or a willingness to think boldly, or a gift for making work fun for the people you manage. In other words, it is the character that you've demonstrated over the course of a thousand transactions that will shape your brand and prompt someone to take a chance on you—or not.

Organizations care tremendously about character because they know that it has everything to do with someone's ability to get a job done well. They also know that if they elevate people whose integrity is spotty or who lack the courage to make difficult decisions, the corporate brand may very well wind up suffering.

> **It's the character you have demonstrated that will decide whether you get the promotions you want—or not.**

In fact, the financial consequences of a key employee's loss of reputation can be devastating for an organization. Consider, for example, the Martha Stewart–ImClone stock trading scandal. In 2002, news broke that Stewart was being investigated for alleged insider trading in the stock of the biotech firm ImClone, whose founder was one of her friends; eventually, she was indicted on charges stemming from that investigation. Among the many corporate scandals of that moment, this one stood out for its purity. Stewart's ImClone trade had nothing to do with her own business, Martha Stewart Living Omnimedia. This was a purely reputational scandal.

Nonetheless, the damage the scandal did to Stewart's personal brand quickly spread to her company's brand as well. The company's stock price fell more than 50 percent in the two months after news of the ImClone investigations broke, and earnings dropped sharply also. The slightest hint that Stewart was willing to cut corners in her personal life made investors, advertisers, and customers lose faith in her business. And not without reason. The list of great organizations brought down by the bad judgment of just a few individuals is long indeed.

Smart organizations have always gone out of their way to look for employees with the kind of personal qualities that will enhance, not compromise, the company's reputation. Now, after watching the personal brands of the top executives of WorldCom, Tyco, Enron, and Adelphia turn to mud and drag down their corporations, even not-so-smart organizations have figured out that they cannot afford to hire and promote people of questionable repute.

> **Smart organizations go out of their way to look for employees who will enhance, not compromise, the company's reputation.**

This means that the single most important thing you can do for your career is to lay the groundwork for an attractive personal reputation, so that the next time someone powerful *does* think of your name, that person thinks well of you.

Of course, building a great personal brand is easier said than done. In fact, it is frequently a great battle. You have to constantly fight the indifference, hostility, cowardliness, and sometimes even mint-eating lunacy of the people with the power to move you forward or hold you back.

> **The single most important thing you can do for your career is to lay the groundwork for an attractive personal reputation.**

You also have to combat your own worst impulses. It's easy to be sloppy and allow the dumb things you say at cocktail parties to influence your brand. It's also easy to be blind to the real moments of truth in a career and to blow them. It's easy to forget that good personal brands are usually built brick by brick and day by day—and that any transaction you have with anyone in a professional capacity has the potential to subtly alter your brand, for better or for worse.

It's also easy to give in to the temptation to take a little shortcut now and then, only to find years down the road that this has cost you everything you've worked for. As hard as you have to fight to build a good brand, you often have to fight even harder to keep it.

Generally, the greatest battles in a career are the battles you have with yourself as you struggle to give the world reasons only to judge you positively. I wrote this book to help ambitious people win those battles and build the kind of name for themselves that will allow them to rise to the level of their ambitions.

This is a natural offshoot of my last book, *Brand Warfare*, in which I offered the basic rules for any corporation that was hoping to establish and build an attractive public personality. And like *Brand Warfare*, this book is not an academic treatise, full of theories derived from scientific studies. Instead, this is the product of 30 years of business experience. The rules are my rules, and they have come out of years of observing—sometimes with admiration and sometimes with stunned disbelief—how people hoping to succeed in organizational life really behave.

Of course, you may very well be wondering whether I wrote this book because I have been infallible in managing my own personal brand.

Definitely not. I have made my share of mistakes over the years and have generated my share of negative news stories. I hope that because I have shot myself in the foot a few times, I can offer you a fuller picture of the struggle to create and maintain a good reputation throughout a career.

People also ask me how I have the time to write, given my day job as CEO of John Hancock Financial Services.

I hate to disappoint any reader who believes that CEOs write every word of their own books themselves, in longhand. Maybe some CEOs do, but I had help with this endeavor. The demands on my time were therefore reasonable. I might also have a few more free hours than most executives because I don't play golf, I don't serve on other for-profit corporate boards, and I don't belong to a rock band.

Instead, I actually find it recreational to organize my ideas on a subject that I am interested in. Since I rose to the CEO's job after beginning my career in marketing and public relations, brand building is something I have given a great deal of thought to over the years. Fortunately, this is an interest that serves the interests of John Hancock very nicely.

In addition, since my profits from both books are assigned to John Hancock, which in turn sends them to charities, I considered writing this book a good way to help raise money for good causes.

Finally, I consider the audience for this book to also be a good cause—good enough that I am willing to accept whatever criticism this work generates in order to give you the unsentimental truth about organizational life.

I have seen too many otherwise talented and capable men and women squander their careers because they were too self-absorbed or arrogant, or failed to project the right personal qualities to people in power, or didn't understand how important it is to treat a receptionist well on any ordinary Monday morning. I don't like to see talent wasted, so I hope to convince you that you are building something important every day with everything you say and everything you do.

It's the brand you make for yourself that determines whether you become mayor of the vertical village—or the village idiot. I wrote this book to help you ensure that the brand you're stuck with is the one you'd give yourself, if you had the choice.

I

TRY TO LOOK BEYOND
YOUR OWN NAVEL

A ny book about personal brands should by rights start with the greatest obstacle of all to building a good one, and that is the extreme self-absorption from which most of us suffer.

In *The Devil's Dictionary*, Ambrose Bierce defines the word "I" this way: "I is the first letter of the alphabet, the first word of the language, the first thought of the mind, the first object of affection."

"I" is certainly the first consideration in organizational life. Most people's reaction to anything that happens in the outfit they work for is, "What about me? Will this be good for me?" For example, the company is suddenly engulfed in scandal. Your first thought is probably not, "How will we get out of this mess?" It's, "Am *I* in trouble?"

Or, you'll hear that management is transferring a division to Arizona. Your immediate thought is not, "Will this be good for the business?" It's, "Would *I* enjoy living in Scottsdale?"

Short of Mother Teresa, very few of us escape seeing the places where we work largely in terms of our own self-interest. However, to build the kind of personal brand that will help you to be successful, you will have to add another filter to the lens. You will have to turn this self-absorption into a desire for self-respect and the respect of the people around you.

> **In order to build a good reputation, you have to view your own actions in the same way that the people judging you will view them.**

You may still be a navel-gazing egotist, but at least you'll be an egotist who recognizes the value of other people's approval.

And in that case, before you say or do anything, you will have to consider whether the move will reflect well upon you. Will it enhance your reputation or tarnish it? Will you be proud of what you've said or done down the road?

In other words, you have to view your own actions in the same way that the people judging you will view them.

DON'T FLATTER YOURSELF

Unfortunately, it is not easy to adopt an external perspective on your own activities, because such a perspective is extremely unnatural. In fact, social psychologists have documented a Grand Canyon–sized gulf between the way in which a person perpetrating an action explains his or her behavior and the way in which outside observers explain it.

The "actor" tends to view the things he or she does as a reaction to external circumstances. For example, if you snap at somebody, you may say to yourself, "I snapped at him only because he drove me to the breaking point." In addition, the actor is very much aware of his or her own intentions in performing an action and is also aware of whether this type of behavior is normal for him or her. You may say to yourself, "Yes, I sounded snappish, but I didn't mean to." Or, "Yes, I did snap at him, but I'm usually a very easy-going person."

Add it all up, and we tend to view our own activities in a very forgiving light. The dog ate the homework, so what could we do?

People who happen to find themselves thrust into some kind of unpleasant spotlight often display this self-forgiving bias. Consider, for example, Darva Conger, the nurse who married a stranger on the 2000 Fox TV show *Who Wants to Marry a Multi-Millionaire?* and then left him shortly thereafter, only to be stunned by an avalanche of bad press.

She told *Good Morning America*, "I am not a gold digger" and "I just want my life back." Then she did the most hypocritical thing of all for someone claiming not to be an opportunist or to like the public attention: She took her clothes off for *Playboy* magazine in return for a substantial payday. But Conger seemed blind to the hypocrisy, arguing instead that her own good intentions excused the *Playboy* spread: "It was my way of poking fun at myself."

Another excellent example of self-forgiveness is Jeffrey Skilling, the former president of Enron. In February 2002, he testified before Congress about the company's collapse. When asked whether he had been aware of the partnership transactions that brought down the company, he blamed external circumstances for his lack of awareness to the point of absurdity. Why did he not hear his CFO promise board members that he would approve these questionable deals? Because the power went out. "The room was dark, quite frankly, and people were walking in and out of the meeting," he said.

To outside observers, on the other hand, the fact that the lights went out during one meeting was hardly material. The problem was Skilling himself, whom one congressman compared to Sergeant Schultz of the old TV show *Hogan's Heroes*, the bumbling Nazi who said, "I see nothing! I hear nothing!"

The truth is that while we tend to view our own less-than-heroic actions as no reflection on the basic goodness of our character, outside observers believe just the opposite: that we do the things we do because of the kind of people we are. After all, they have far less information than we do about our actions. They have no idea that we met a dog on the way who ate our homework, or that we didn't really intend to have our homework be eaten, or that we've never had our homework eaten before. As far as the outside observer is concerned—particularly one who does not know us very well—we don't have our homework because we're the kind of unreliable personality whose homework *does* get eaten.

> **Everyone has a natural tendency to make excuses for their behavior. Don't make excuses for yours. People will decide who you are on the basis of the things you do.**

Social psychologists call this tendency of outside observers to assume that internal attributes are the cause of every action "the fundamental attribution error." It may be an error of perception, but it is also a fact of life. Everything you do and say will be viewed by the people around you as evidence of *who you are*.

Actually, this tendency to interpret other people's actions in terms of their basic character is extremely useful. It adds some sense of control and predictability to the chaotic world of human relations. Person A may decide whether Person B is trustworthy based on very little information—but once A has labeled B, A has the comfort of knowing what to expect from B and is able to adjust his or her own behavior accordingly.

And once A's assessment of B becomes common wisdom within his or her organization, everybody in the office feels as if he or she is on solid ground with B as well. Person B now has a recognizable brand.

Once, when I was young and in the public relations business, I witnessed an example of stunningly rapid brand building that immediately told my entire firm how to handle one of its clients. The client was a wine vintner's group, and I was such a minor player at that point that it was my job to make sure that the head of the wine group and his wife were comfortable when they came to New York City.

Since they were staying in an incredible suite at the Plaza, you'd think this would have been easy. But this was at a time when the domestic wine industry was still insecure regarding the French, and, maybe as a result, this couple was imperious beyond belief. The guy behaved as if he had been born into the wine business as a Rothschild, instead of having been hired into it as the PR person for a trade organization. And his consort was worse.

We were given a long list of her requirements. One of the things she insisted on was that there be no footprints on the carpet when they entered the hotel room. I'm not talking about dirt; I'm talking about indentations. Since we were constantly in their suite, trying to provide the many amenities they demanded, we were endlessly calling housekeeping and persuading the poor confused chambermaids to vacuum the plush carpet while walking backwards out of the room.

The most specific of the wine woman's requirements involved the light she needed in the bathroom in order to properly apply her makeup. The sheet I received actually specified a setting on a light meter. So I dutifully went over there with a light meter, trying to figure out whether to add or subtract lamps and makeup mirrors.

I guess I don't know how to read a light meter, because there was *not* enough light in the room. Never mind that there was neither enough light nor enough makeup in all of Bloomingdale's to make this woman attractive. She caused a ruckus beyond belief because she had been handicapped in her makeup application, and she insisted that there be a reprimand. So, I was yelled at by the higher-ups.

The story spread like wildfire within my firm. Within a day, no one in that office who had any talent was willing to do anything for this client. The better people all said, "I won't work on the account," and they got away with it because they had choices. As I said, personal brands are definitely useful—for the really good employees, there was now one less client to worry about.

Though the wine people were an extreme example, they were suffering from a disease that frequently holds people back in their working lives: What they saw when they looked in the mirror in no way corresponded to external reality. They thought they resembled Prince Rainier and Princess Grace of Monaco. We saw Nicolae and Elena Ceausescu of Romania—petty despots with no culture and a monstrous appetite for luxury.

Of course, developing an accurate self-image is always a struggle. None of us is as benevolent, intelligent, or impressive as we believe—or, for that matter, as the people who want to flatter us would have us believe.

But if you can't begin to look at yourself with some detachment, you will never be able to alter your behavior so that it corresponds to the kind of person you would ideally like to be. Instead, you will be the professional equivalent of poor Darva Conger, moving from embarrassment to embarrassment, denying all the while that these embarrassments express anything significant about you.

> **Don't flatter yourself. You can't build a good personal brand if you can't see yourself as others see you.**

In fact, being able to peel back the layer of denial that keeps us from understanding our own behavior is such a huge advantage in professional life that I am all for acquiring that knowledge in any way you can. You can read great novels, or you can consult your wise Uncle Eddie. I'm a big believer in shrinks—good shrinks, not the kind that get employed by corporations—to give you insight into what motivates you to act the way you do. With any luck, they will also give you something else just as valuable: insight into why other people behave as bizarrely as they do.

Above all, be aware that your behavior defines you. Since you are going to be judged not on your intentions and desires, but rather on your external actions, try not to develop tunnel vision. Consider things beyond your own self-interest, such as the well-being of the people you work with and the organization you work for.

GET NOTICED

Once you have become self-aware enough to shape your behavior, where do you go from there?

Obviously, in order to establish a reputation with the powerful people in your organization, you first have to be noticed by them. This is not always easy.

Let me tell you about the first time I really got the attention of someone powerful.

It was my first job out of school. I was working at a big New York City communications firm and suffering every humiliation you can possibly suffer at the beginning of a career. I was barely able to live on my salary. After paying my rent and other bills, I would literally have $5 for the weekend. I owned two pairs of dress slacks and one sports coat. That was my wardrobe. I had a secretary who refused to type for me because she was making $11,000 and I was making just $10,800.

And, to top it off, one day, when I'd been there only a few months, I was told to come to the boss's boss's office at 6 p.m. Obviously, I was about to be fired. That was the time of day people got fired at that firm. They never fired people first thing in the morning. If they had to pay you for the day, they wanted to make sure that they got a full day's work out of you.

Besides, what other reason would the head of the office have for wanting to see me? The guy was so uptight and so "my-ancestors-came-over-on-the-Mayflower" superior that we used to call him Mr. Stiff. Mr. Stiff and I had barely exchanged a word during my short tenure.

His behavior that evening only confirmed my suspicion that I was getting the ax. At the end of a long workday, he did not invite me to sit.

He had me stand in front of his desk as if it were the military. My stomach churned.

Mr. Stiff finally opened his mouth, and as I waited for the blade to fall, he did something very strange. He offered me a promotion and matter-of-factly said, "I'm going to raise your salary to $12,000."

Twelve thousand dollars! I thought it was incredible. Now my secretary would *have* to type for me! I wanted to express my joy and gratitude and relief, but, in all honesty, I was still feeling a little queasy.

I wasn't sure if it was nerves or the scrod I'd had for lunch at the Captain's Table. I hadn't eaten fish since I was a child, ever since my mother had fried up the family goldfish for my dinner. Of course, I was the one who'd fished the goldfish out of the tank, in retaliation for not being allowed to go on a fishing trip with my older brother. The smell of fried fish had haunted me for years, but this was the day that I thought I'd finally give seafood another try.

Unfortunately, this was not the best time to discover that I was actually allergic to fish. Then it happened.

I was trying to concentrate on the prospect of a hundred extra dollars a month, when all of a sudden, I retched—just straight at him, with incredible force, all over his desk, his papers, his beautiful gray flannel suit. Linda Blair of *The Exorcist* was a piker compared to me.

He was too repressed to mention the fact that I had just *vomited* on him. I think he thought it was some Italian negotiating technique he was unfamiliar with.

His reaction was so peculiar that it actually saved me from feeling too bad about what I'd just done. I was outraged by his coldness. Did he ask me to sit down? Did he offer to call a doctor? Did he get angry? No. I would have taken anger over the complete lack of emotion and concern.

Despite the raise and the promotion, Mr. Stiff clearly had yet to see me as a human being. This incident gave me a little insight: My bosses were not about to launch a voyage of discovery to learn about me. To them, I was a tool. And, as a tool, I had better find ways to distinguish myself, aside from throwing up.

The fact is, Mr. Stiff's attitude is not uncommon. You may be barely real to the people above you in an organization if you don't find a way to improve their lives. So, the single best way to establish a personal brand when you are new to an organization is by becoming useful—ideally, uniquely useful. Be smart. Stake out your own territory by finding something that the organization is missing that you can provide.

That is exactly what I did with Mr. Stiff, and I soon became indispensable to him.

First, I took my youth and inexperience and turned it into something that had value. I became known as the young "idea" guy to whom you could hand any project and he would come up with a number of ideas to move the project forward. This was important in that office because the middle-aged people I was surrounded by were short

> **The best way to establish a brand when you are new to an organization is by offering something that the organization is missing.**

on ideas. They all wanted to be philosophers, wise men who edited other people's ideas. Soon, there was no new business pitch in that office that didn't include me.

Second, I became a source of news that people could not do without. These were the days when breaking news came in, not over the Internet or cable TV, but over a Dow Jones Teletype that left reams of paper on the floor. I volunteered to do something incredibly simple: I would leave my office every 30 minutes or so, cut the Teletype, and post the stories on a bulletin board. My peers thought this

> **To get noticed, turn whatever particular qualities you offer into something that is of value to the higher-ups.**

task was far too menial for them, but it put me on the radar.

Since I got to monitor the news related to our clients first, I could poke my head into my boss's office or another account head's office and say, "By the way, Engelhard Industries just announced it is going to buy tons of platinum from Russia." The higher-ups could then jump on the phone, call their clients, and look as if they were paying incredible attention to them.

The truth is, the powerful people in any organization have plenty of volunteers to take on the high-profile, high-status assignments. Sometimes the smartest thing you can do is take on a humble task that needs doing.

The third thing I did to establish myself was to become the way to get a reservation at the finest restaurants in the country. This was quite an ironic development for an Italian-American kid from upstate New York who until that point had never eaten in a two-star restaurant,

> **There are probably plenty of volunteers for every high-profile task, so sometimes the best way to be noticed by those in power is to do something humble but essential.**

let alone a five-star. But I took on an account called the Mobil Travel Guides, which rated restaurants. Mobil had this incredibly great-looking award that it would give to the restaurants that won its top ranking, but it had never really publicized it properly.

I convinced Mobil to do a series of press releases and features when it awarded any restaurant five stars. Then I got the food critics from the local television stations to come in and do these three- or four-minute bits with the owner and the chef. Even in New York City, we got tremendous publicity, and publicity is extremely hard for restaurants to come by, given the intense competition they face. So I came away with tremendous gratitude from the owners and chefs of the top restaurants around the country.

As a result, I never had any trouble getting a restaurant reservation anywhere. Soon, my bosses figured out that the way to get into a restaurant that was impossible to get into—La Grenouille, La Côte Basque, Lutèce, The Four Seasons—was through me. With clients, it was very impressive. If they were from out of town, their spouse was with them, and they were hoping for a romantic dinner at one of the best restaurants in New York, I could always say, "No problem. Where do you want to go?"

And when you walk into Lutèce and you're 22 years old and legendary proprietor André Soltner comes over and greets you, but doesn't greet your boss until you introduce the two of them and make them both feel important—that is something.

If you have the opportunity, try to take advantage of what marketers call "the halo effect." Associate your brand with something glamorous and valuable, and by extension, you will become valuable, too.

Of course, my early achievements in terms of the halo effect were minimal compared to those of Virgin Group founder Richard Branson. As a 17-year-old boy, Branson turned a brush with glamour into an empire.

> **Associate your brand with something glamorous and valuable, and you will become valuable, too.**

He and a friend founded a magazine in London called *Student* with nothing more than nerve. Somehow they got the hip young actress Vanessa Redgrave—who must have been a very good sport indeed—to agree to talk with them.

"The interview was a turning point for us," Branson wrote in his book *Losing My Virginity*, "since we could now use her name as a magnet to attract other contributors." Suddenly, Branson was interviewing Mick Jagger and John Lennon and convincing advertisers who were eager to reach a young audience that they should send money his way. He was barely shaving, but he was now a player in the world of entertainment.

> **When you are young, getting access to powerful people is the name of the game.**

When you are young, getting access to powerful people is the name of the game. If you gain access to power early, you will learn an enormous amount very quickly—and you will put yourself in an entirely different category from your peers who communicate with these people only through a hierarchy.

BECOME A PRODUCT WITH THE RIGHT FEATURES

Of course, getting the positive notice of powerful people is only the first step. You want them not just to appreciate you where you are, but also to move you up. And for that, you will have to develop a brand that shouts "upward mobility."

How do you do that?

At the risk of appalling all the humanists out there, I can tell you that it's smart for you to try to think of yourself as a product—an expensive one—because at the end of the day, that's exactly what you are to your organization, to your boss, and to your customers. You probably cost them as much every year as a top-of-the-line Mercedes, and that's how they think of you, too. And you'd better deliver the performance they expect from a luxury brand, because who wants an unreliable Mercedes?

No one.

When it comes to luxury sedans, cheap upholstery and poor pickup will not cut it. When it comes to employees, certain things are simply not negotiable if they are going to be considered for higher office.

It doesn't matter whether you work in the software industry or the steel industry; or whether you aspire to Warren Buffett's folksy common sense or Phil Knight of Nike's "bad to the bone" attitude. If you expect to go far, you have to develop a reputation for five key qualities:

- Earning the organization money
- Telling the truth
- Being discreet
- Keeping your promises
- Making people want to work for you

If you are missing any one of these qualities, you don't have the right kind of brand for a big career, and it is highly unlikely that anyone will consider you executive-office material.

Let's consider these brand cornerstones one by one.

BECOME FAMOUS FOR BRINGING HOME THE BEAR

Organizational life is not that different from life among the cavemen. There are the hunters and the trappers, the skinners, and the cooks, as well as the engineering geniuses who invented the clubs and snares used by the hunters and the trappers. This last group, the engineers, is frequently a little bitter, because they think they never get enough credit for their inventions. If it weren't for them, they believe, the tribe would not be able to eat.

In fact, everyone considers his or her function to be the most essential. For example, the skinners—the cave equivalent of a corporation's financial types—truly believe that cutting up the meat and divvying it up trumps all other functions. If they had their way, no one would spend any money on bows and arrows or clubs. They'd just put all the tribe's resources into weighing the meat more precisely.

Yet, the greatest respect in cave society invariably goes to one type of caveman: the hunters and trappers who bring home the bear. In other words, those who make money for the corporation or bring in donations for the nonprofit rise first.

It is always smart, therefore, to make your way at some point or other into a production or development job where you can be credited directly for beautifying the bottom line. Especially when you are young, being a successful hunter can give you a huge advantage over your peers.

You know, I played on my high school football team one year. I remember one night when we had just lost a game and were on the bus coming back late.

A lot of the people in the bus were chattering. Suddenly, the quarterback spoke up: "Look, the only guys who should be talking are the guys who played. Guys who didn't play, don't talk."

A lot of organizations have the same attitude. If you are young and unaccomplished, no one wants to hear from you—unless, of course, you become a starter in one of three ways:

- By offering such incredible wisdom, skill, ideas, or connections that the higher-ups need you immediately in a *consigliere* role
- By being the boss's kid or in-law
- By the most likely route—selling your way into people's notice

If you are generating a lot of revenue for an organization, the people in charge simply have to listen to you.

You are also less likely to be fired or laid off if you are a hunter. That's why there are so many obnoxious salespeople in the world: People who can sell are retained even if their personality defects are numerous. Just as in the tribes of old, hunters are allowed to be unshaven and crude and unkempt.

Of course, none of this means that you cannot rise to the upper ranks of your organization from the club-inventing or meat-weighing side of the business. But in that case, you'll have to become skilled at getting the people who *work for you* to bring home the bear.

You also have to demonstrate faith in the bear-hunting abilities of the entire tribe. I frequently offer the junior executives at my firm a choice: a higher guaranteed salary or a lower guarantee but a greater potential upside linked to our performance. Anyone who chooses the higher guarantee is going nowhere.

> **To be considered for the upper ranks, get into a position where you are making money for your organization.**

CONVINCE PEOPLE THAT YOU RESEMBLE GEORGE WASHINGTON—YOU CANNOT TELL A LIE

Dishonesty is fatal in business, and for good reason. Trust is the oil that greases the wheels of commerce.

As early as 1766, political economist Adam Smith noticed that scrupulous honesty and a thriving business went hand in hand. "Of all the nations in Europe," he wrote, "the Dutch, the most commercial, are the most faithful to their word."

Smith observed that it was specifically *because* their businesses were so wide-ranging and active that Dutch merchants knew that they could not afford a dent in their reputations. "When a person makes perhaps twenty contracts in a day . . . the very appearance of a cheat would make him lose," Smith wrote.

Over 200 years later, eBay operates a vibrant online marketplace on the exact same principle. Buyers are able to trust sellers that they do not know and cannot visit because other buyers in the past have posted feedback about them on the site. And the more active the seller, and the more feedback he or she has collected, the more likely he or she is to jealously guard the quality of that feedback, and the more trustworthy he or she is likely to be.

An active seller cannot afford to fleece even a single customer. At "the very appearance of a cheat," thousands of potential customers would flee.

The truth is, when you have a thriving business, the risks of dishonesty tend to far outweigh any potential profit you might gain from it. Any funny business, and the resulting exodus of customers and investors can shrink a big operation into a small one in a matter of weeks. Just consider how rapidly the market capitalization of WorldCom and Enron collapsed after the dishonesty of their accounting was revealed.

All this means one simple thing for you: Any organization you are going to want to work for will consider dishonest people a risk that it cannot bear.

Fortunately, I learned how seriously good organizations take even a little white lie very early in my career. When I was 23, I wanted a job so badly that I said on my résumé that I was 25. I thought they would want someone older. It didn't make a lot of sense.

I got the job. Then, as I was filling out the paperwork for Personnel, I saw that practically every form asked me for my birthdate. To my horror, I discovered that I was going to have to lie again and again and again.

I had a profound revelation: Little white lies can haunt you. If I persisted in this lie, I would wind up living it for a long time.

I'd already accepted this job and had quit my old one. But I knew that I'd made a terrible mistake. So I called my boss-to-be, a smart, decent guy named Traug Keller, and told him the humiliating truth, recognizing that it might cost me the job.

Traug was very concerned. He said he'd have to think about it and call me back.

He called me the next day. He was still unhappy, but he had discussed the matter with his boss. And because I'd come forward and admitted what I had done, they were going to take me on. However, they wanted to put me on notice that one more lie at that level, and I would be fired.

Traug, who went on to become one of the great mentors in my career, saved me from oblivion at that particular moment. He also kept me from winding up like Sandy Baldwin, the former president of the United States Olympic Committee, who was disgraced for lying about her educational accomplishments, or George O'Leary, briefly the football coach for Notre Dame, who resigned after admitting that he had glorified both his academic background and his college football career. Both of them had been carrying around their little white lies for *two decades*—until they were successful enough for it to be worth someone's while to look into the truth of their curriculum vitae, and they were caught.

> **A reputation for dishonesty is a career-ender.**

I'm sure those résumé-boosting lies were helpful when they were first used. However, no matter what a lie wins you in the short term, it is not worth the cost to your career in the long term.

Tell your assistant that her new haircut looks great even when it doesn't, but do not perjure yourself when it comes to your job. No amount of talent, brains, or accomplishments will save you if you do.

BECOME FAMOUS FOR YOUR GARBO-ESQUE SILENCE

Somebody recently said to me, "Information is power only if you can pass it on."

This seems to me to be a particularly naïve way to look at information. Frequently, it offers more of an advantage when you *don't* pass it on, when you simply keep something to yourself that you and you alone are able to act on.

That is one great argument for discretion.

The second great argument is that if you are indiscreet, no one with any power will trust you. While it's enjoyable to gossip, especially about colleagues you don't like, I've seen enough people damage their reputations by saying something in public that they shouldn't have said, to believe that it is frequently smarter to keep your own counsel.

As you might guess, this was one lesson I had to learn the hard way.

For example, I once had a boss whom I considered a complete nincompoop. And when I was told that I wasn't going to be working for him anymore, I actually made the mistake of informing him how glad I was—without reservation.

Lo and behold, three years later, I was reassigned to him. His memory was particularly keen, and he made my life miserable. All of a sudden, my expense reports were gone over with a fine-toothed comb. I had no authority to sign bills anymore. All my ideas were unworthy. It was like having your ex-mother-in-law for your boss. Absolute torture, two full years of it, as punishment for five minutes of enjoyment in telling him off.

Fortunately, however, with this particular instance of tactlessness, I did little more than hurt myself.

If that were all that were at stake—a little personal embarrassment, a bit of a decline in personal reputation for those who talk out of school—no one would consider discretion a particularly important quality. But that is not all that is at stake. If you are the type of person who routinely says more than he or she should and says it in the wrong place to the wrong people, you could wind up costing your company a tremendous amount of money and respect.

For example, John Hancock once had a good relationship with a nationally acclaimed consulting company that was doing $7 million worth of business with us every year. This was a very strong group, and they had infiltrated our organization like locusts. Every time you opened a door, there was another one of them.

Then one day, the consulting company held an off-site seminar for its senior partners, and someone lower down in the organization did a very smart presentation in which he called two or three of Hancock's top executives idiots and laid out a plan for taking advantage of our stupidity. The idea was to move from $7 million a year in fees to $12 million without a corresponding increase in the consulting company's costs. The guy expected to go from a 28 percent margin to a 50 percent margin.

And he had thoughtfully provided hard copies of his presentation for all attending. Sure enough, someone forgot the thing under his or her chair, and the person who found it posted it on the Internet, from whence it made its way to us. The best part was, the then-chairman of John Hancock learned that his high-priced consultants thought he was a moron.

A mistake. The chairman was both brilliant and tough.

I told him I would take care of it.

So, I called in the most senior partner in the firm, not the partner who had prepared the presentation. He arrived at my office, we gave him some coffee, and he settled in complacently, sure that we were going to give him the extra $5 million in business that his company wanted. Instead, he received a gasoline enema, and he rocketed out of there, having learned that he had lost every penny of the $7 million the company was already getting.

Sometimes the cost of saying too much is even greater than that. For example, the CEO of Cerner Corp. sent his company's stock price down 21 percent in just three days in 2001 by venting indiscreetly at his employees in an email. Complaining that the parking lot was too empty and employees were not working long enough hours, he wrote, "Hell will freeze over before this CEO implements ANOTHER EMPLOYEE benefit in this Culture." He went on, "What you are doing, as managers, with this company makes me SICK." Thanks to its hysterical language, the email was ripe for an Internet posting. And it immediately made investors want to dump the stock.

While the temptation to be indiscreet probably goes back to cave times, we live in an age in which the chance that any indiscretion will go unpunished are slim and getting slimmer. Technology allows your thoughtless words to be snatched out of the air and turned from a private communication into a mass release with ease.

The indiscreet voicemails that you leave, for example, can be broadcast to anyone in your organization—something that happened to me once when a colleague who didn't like me as much as she might have "accidentally" pushed the wrong button on her phone.

And the indiscreet memos that you write can be posted within hours on web sites like www.InternalMemos.com that exist just to make internal communications very public indeed.

And the indiscreet emails that you bang out not only are easily forwarded to the universe and easily eavesdropped on by your bosses, but also are easily retrieved even after they are erased. History has shown that they can be used by regulators and prosecutors to cause you and your organization a heap of trouble.

One of the problems with email in particular is that it's quick and solitary, and it encourages bravado. People tend to say things in an email that they would never say in person. Try to avoid the temptation to be a paper tiger. Do not write or record anything that you would not want to have subpoenaed or published.

> Indiscretions can cost an organization a great deal, so become known for your excellent judgment about when to speak and when to keep quiet.

Ultimately, the organizational costs of a single indiscretion can be so high—you can derail a merger, ruin your company's brand, cost your CEO his or her job—that if you gain a reputation for being indiscreet, you may as well pack it up. You will have no career worth having. If, on the other hand, you gain a reputation as someone who can keep a secret and has good judgment about when to speak and when to be reticent, powerful people will want you around.

WIN A NAME AS THE HUMAN EQUIVALENT OF FEDEX: ALWAYS DELIVER ON TIME

Like discretion and honesty, delivering on your promises is a trust issue. If you overpromise and underdeliver, you won't be trusted by your bosses, and you will go nowhere. If you say, "I will make this sales goal," you simply have to do it, by any legal and ethical means.

In fact, the judicious use of promises that you *can* deliver on can propel you up the ladder faster than anything except bringing home the bear. Promising to do something that your more timid peers think cannot be done will distinguish you from the pack, provided that you deliver.

Can you do things that other people cannot do? That's one of the questions that determines how high you rise.

For example, I once made a promise to a boss I had in the advertising business that I knew would require a lot of delicacy and thought to keep. One of the boss's best friends worked for the agency and was not performing. They had been in each other's weddings, but he had to go.

I promised the boss that I would take care of it in such a way that his friend would not blame him.

I called in the friend. He was very cocky because he had such a close relationship with the boss.

"So what job am I getting with you?" he asked.

"You don't have a job," I said.

He was astonished.

I explained my problems with his work ethic and went on. "If you fight me on this," I said, "I will give you the standard severance deal, and that's it. But if you accept my decision, I will give you twice that deal."

Then I added, "If you decide to go the boss and complain, you'll have to take the risk that he won't back you up. And even if he does, you'll last only until I rise high enough to overrule him. And then the quality of the severance deal will be a lot lower than what I'm offering you today."

He weighed the odds and took the deal.

So the guy got to save face—he simply said to the boss that he'd decided to leave. The boss looked good, too, because everybody knew it was time for this guy to go, even though it would be hard for him personally.

> To quickly elevate your personal brand, make bold promises and deliver on them.

Because I was willing to be the bad guy in the situation, I had kept my promise and had risen in the estimation of someone who held my career in his hands.

The two men are still friends today. And the friend still thinks I am a jerk, a cross I seem to be willing to bear.

BECOME KNOWN AS THE COACH THE PLAYERS WANT TO PLAY FOR

Almost everyone starts his or her career managing a simple task. Then you get to manage more than one task, and people start calling these tasks projects. After a while, you come to manage people who manage projects. It's at that point that *people* become your project.

Eventually, you will wind up managing people across different disciplines, often disciplines that you have no familiarity with. Then you

are really into exponential management. At that point, your ability to do
things yourself is relatively meaning-
less. Your ability to get things done
through others becomes what you're
getting paid for.

> You have to develop a reputation for leadership, because at some point your ability to do things yourself becomes meaningless. What counts is whether you can get other people to do them.

And the difference between what
can be accomplished by a group of people who are willing to do only the minimum and a group of people who are
willing to go the extra mile for you is
enormous. The recent history of the Boston Celtics offers an excellent
example. A talented team had three and a half losing seasons under
coach Rick Pitino. Pitino had been a legendary college basketball
coach, but many people believed that his micromanaging, overbearing
style backfired with self-respecting adults. It appeared that the players
just would not play for him.

Pitino left mid-season in 2001, and his assistant, Jim O'Brien, took
over. In O'Brien's first full season, the team made it to the NBA's
Eastern Conference Finals for the first time in 14 years. The apparent
difference was, O'Brien treated the players like collaborators, not like
errant children, and they were willing to give their all for him. Celtics
guard Tony Delk told the press, "Coach O'Brien shows us respect and,
in turn, we show it to him."

People above you will notice whether your team is willing to play
for you. You will never rise as far as you want to if you do not develop a
reputation for leadership.

Unfortunately, few things are more difficult to acquire. The most
complex undertaking that anyone faces in a career is managing other
people. There is only one thing in life that is more complex, and that
is raising children. The difference is, the people at work *have* to listen
to you.

I am the last person who would call himself a great manager, but I have learned a few simple rules about leading a team that seem to help:

First, it's about the people, not the theory. While I find the many management theories out there interesting—the "One-Minute Manager," management by walking around, total quality management—the best managers are not the most brilliant strategists. They are the people who have figured out how to get the most out of what is probably a highly diverse group of players. My advice is, try to look at the people you manage as individuals. They all need to be motivated differently. With some people, you'll need a whip, a gun, and a chair. With other people, it's sugar cubes and schmoozing. Flexibility is a sign of leadership.

Second, know what you don't know. It's not your job to be an expert on everything, and you will never be effective if you insist on pretending that you are. Instead of trying to teach all your subordinates how to do their jobs, it is far smarter to hire people with great skills who will teach you something and can give you advice and counsel on matters you know nothing about. Recognize that you will need people with expertise in many different areas. Recognize also that this is unlikely to be a homogeneous group, and make sure that you don't surround yourself with people who walk and talk just like you. Recognize also that not everybody who works for you is necessarily someone you would want to take home for dinner.

> **Here are a few simple ideas for adding leadership to your brand:**
> - **It's about the people, not the theory.**
> - **Know what you don't know.**
> - **A reputation for fairness is everything.**

Third, a reputation for fairness is everything. Before people will really show you what they can do, you have to inspire trust and confidence. You have to listen to them, value their ideas, and treat them respectfully. You have to prove to them that if they do a great job for you, they will be recognized and rewarded for it. And fairness on your part becomes more meaningful to them the higher you rise and the more power you have to be *un*fair.

The formula for a successful personal brand is pretty simple: Become self-aware. Get noticed by people in power. Develop qualities that suggest that you are going places.

Here is what is not simple: convincing your immediate boss to give you the opportunity to demonstrate those attractive qualities.

In the next chapter, I will lay out the basic rules of conduct for the most significant and fraught relationship in your working life: the relationship you have with your boss—that frequently problematic person who gives you your assignments, reviews your accomplishments, decides how much you are worth monetarily, and largely determines how you are seen by the organization at large.

RULE

$$\boxed{2}$$

LIKE IT OR NOT, YOUR BOSS IS THE COAUTHOR OF YOUR BRAND

Accept the fact that you have to pay your dues in organizational life. For most of your career, you can expect your bosses to take credit for your ideas, exploit your energy, siphon off the positive attention your efforts attract, and, just to top things off, demand various amounts of ring kissing from you. You may very well spend most of your career "making rain" and bringing vast amounts of money into your organization while the men and women on top take the lion's share out. You pay your dues again and again.

That is the way organizations work. The elders of the tribe eat first. If you

> **Accept the fact that you have to pay your dues. Early in your career, you will be making most of the money for the organization and expending most of the sweat, while the senior people reap most of the rewards.**

cannot accept that, there is only one thing to do: Start your own organization, so that you'll be at the top of the food chain.

Otherwise, you simply cannot fight the power structure. And deciding to try to fight it is exceptionally dangerous, because no one has more influence over the quality of your life than your boss—not even, I would argue, your significant other.

Your boss generally has much more to say about your life than your spouse does because your boss commands more of your waking time, and probably more of your attention, too. Add up the hours you spend with your boss, or spend thinking about your boss, or spend wishing you had a different boss. If your spouse were as psychically demanding as this, chances are you would already be divorced.

Your boss also determines how much money you make, what kind of experience you gain, how much authority you have, what the next step of your career will be, and whether you'll be posted to Paris, France, or Paris, Maine.

And, if your boss commands any kind of respect within your organization, he or she has the most significant kind of control over your future. *To a great extent, your boss controls your personal brand.*

Within the world of people who can actually advance your career, your image is almost entirely in your boss's hands. This is because organizations are caste systems. Assistant vice presidents talk to assistant vice presidents. Vice presidents talk to vice presidents. Senior vice presidents talk to senior vice presidents. And whatever the level your boss is at, he or she is probably talking about *you* to his or her peers.

The separation between the castes means that your accomplishments may win you one kind of reputation among your subordinates and colleagues, and another one entirely in the boss empire. There, among the pooh-bahs, your personal brand is usually less dependent on any objective evidence of your success or failure, and more dependent on the subjective things your superior is saying about you.

For example, if you accomplish something terrific, and your boss feels grateful to you and wants to push you along, he or she might spin the accomplishment this way: "It was her idea. She really got the team behind her, and she just did a great job."

If, on the other hand, the boss does not like you, or is insecure in the face of your abilities, or even is afraid to lose you, he or she may spin the achievement this way: "It was a great idea, but it really wasn't hers. Some of the other guys came up with it, and she took it and ran with it—but I can't tell you how hard it was to get this one done. She's not without talent, but given the resources she used and the number of people she pissed off, I'm not sure it was worth it."

People can be undercut pretty quickly that way. And if I am an uninvolved peer of your boss, *my* impression of your latest year's work will be based on nothing more than that conversation.

That's true power. You did the same job either way. But the boss determines how it is talked about, and therefore the degree to which you'll be rewarded for it.

Even if your boss is like some of the bosses I've had in my career—an idiot whose abilities are illusory—this power is completely real and has to be respected. So, it behooves you to manage the relationship intelligently, no matter who your boss is.

> **Your boss decides how your accomplishments will be viewed by the higher-ups. Even if he or she is an idiot, the power is real, so handle him or her carefully.**

This isn't always easy. In my case, it was often extremely difficult. I have always had one objective in my life: to have the fewest people possible in a position to make me do something I don't want to do. Being told what to do has always felt unnatural to me.

But the boss relationship is almost inescapable. Even entrepreneurs have to answer to their venture capitalists and CEOs to their boards and shareholders.

The first step toward managing that relationship intelligently is to consider it from the boss's point of view. Let's borrow a phrase from Freud: What do bosses want?

They want you to do your job well, of course. But there's an assumption that you know what you're doing. That's what allows you to keep the job. It will take other qualities if you intend to develop the kind of name that will allow you to move up.

> **Bosses want three things:**
> - **Loyalty**
> - **Good advice**
> - **To have their personal brands polished**

The really relevant question is whether or not the boss trusts you.

BOSSES WANT LOYALTY

More than anything else, bosses want loyalty—not blind loyalty, but an appropriate form of loyalty. That is because most bosses, down deep, are frightened. At three o'clock in the morning, when their eyes snap open, most of them cannot believe they have gotten as far as they have. Now, during the daytime, they actually think they are supposed to be in the driver's seat. But in the middle of the night, they're not so sure. So, they want to make sure that the people who report to them are not trying to do them in.

This means that except for chasing the boss's wife or husband, the fastest method of suicide in organizational life is talking negatively about your boss to others. Everybody knows the saying, "Hell hath no fury like a woman scorned." Well, there is one topper for that: Hell *really* hath no fury like a boss scorned. Your boss will find a way to take you out. And even your peers, while they may encourage that kind of talk, will use it against you. After all, it is to their advantage if the aquarium has fewer fish.

I've seen it happen thousands of times. For example, I once worked with a guy—let's call him "Doug"—who actually did a fantastic job of selling the corporation's services all over the country. But he gained a reputation for going around his boss and telling his boss's boss how much he had done, even to the point of badmouthing his boss.

> **Hell hath no fury like a boss scorned. Do not talk negatively about your boss to your coworkers.**

Doug was terrific at his job. But he did not understand how power worked. And—surprise, surprise—he ended up getting transferred suddenly to the international division, which promptly sent him to some obscure corner of the world, a place from which he never reemerged. He had worked years for a promotion, only to be drop-kicked to another planet.

Doug clearly didn't understand that badmouthing his boss put him in a race against time. Before his boss could get to him, he needed to get his boss's boss to acknowledge that he was more important than his boss. And that didn't happen.

In fact, in case you are tempted to try the same thing, it almost never happens. And not just because the boss's boss is not necessarily going to be interested in tearing down the hierarchy just for your benefit. But also because he or she is aware that if you have willingly betrayed one superior, you will have no compunction about someday betraying him or her as well. You are branded a dangerous character in the eyes of the higher-ups.

> **Beware of complaining about your boss to his or her boss. You will develop a reputation for disloyalty that senior executives will hold against you.**

This means that even if your boss is barely worthy of respect, you will have to give him or her a certain degree of loyalty for as long as you are interested in holding the job.

Of course, the bosses who are *most* worthy of respect are the ones who are secure enough not to demand a tremendous show of loyalty to them personally. Instead, they will demand that you demonstrate loyalty to the organization.

BOSSES WANT GOOD ADVICE

Good advice is extremely hard to come by because the kinds of people who are capable of giving it are relatively rare in organizational life.

> **There are three types of corporate personalities:**
> - **Sycophants**
> - **Contrarians**
> - **Balanced players**

Whether they know it or not, all intelligent bosses instinctively separate the people they manage into three distinct categories: the sycophants, the contrarians, and the small percentage of their employees who are the balanced players. Only the balanced players offer any advice worth listening to. And if your boss has any common sense, only the balanced players will get the opportunity to rise.

Let's consider these three different types of corporate personalities and the pitfalls of being branded the wrong one.

THE SYCOPHANTS: DON'T BE IGOR

In my experience, about 70 percent of the people in any organization are sycophants.

Of course, most of them don't *know* that they are sycophants. They rationalize to themselves that they are indeed not suck-ups. I'm sure they go home to their husbands and wives and brag about how they stood up to the boss. And they can be quite clever at disguising their sycophancy—at least from themselves. These are the people who constantly say, "Well, boss, most of the time I wouldn't agree with you on a matter like this, but I have to this time."

And the fact of the matter is, they *always* agree with the boss. They agree for the sake of agreeing.

Why are they so craven? Because it is a way to win the protection of somebody stronger than they are—or at least to avoid his or her overt hostility.

Extreme sycophancy has been observed in animals as well, particularly in wolves and apes in captivity, where the weaker cannot escape the frustrated energies of the stronger. A weaker wolf may passively roll over on its back when stronger wolves come near, or may demonstrate extreme friendliness toward the stronger wolves, wagging its tail so determinedly that its entire hindquarters sway. Scientist L. David Mech describes the posture that these sycophantic wolves adopt toward their superiors as an "active lack of challenge." That is a pretty good description of the behavior of those weaker animals in corporate captivity as well.

Extremes of submissiveness actually have been documented in human beings under stress. Consider, for example, the famous Stockholm syndrome, a psychological phenomenon in which hostages become strangely sympathetic to the people victimizing them. The most famous American victim of Stockholm syndrome was Patty Hearst, the newspaper heiress who was kidnapped in 1974 by a radical group that called itself the Symbionese Liberation Army. After being terrorized and humiliated by them, she took up their cause and wound up helping them rob a bank.

Many corporate people become sycophants because they, too, are suffering from Stockholm syndrome. They're so insecure that they can't help themselves—it's more pleasant to agree with everything the boss says than to face the fear of what the boss could do to them if displeased.

Other corporate people are sycophants not because they are actively terrified, but because they are naturally conservative and risk-averse. And you *are* more likely to stay alive in the corporate world if you agree with everything your boss says. You will get the longest run out of it. So these people have made a decision that they are content to get by. They have basically decided that they're members of a union, the Sycophants' Union.

Their quest is to remain unnoticed, for the most part. So long as they are reasonably proficient at their jobs and keep their heads down, they are less likely to be called out of class than someone who speaks his or her mind. They want the kind of career where they will be rewarded with a 3 percent pay increase each year, good benefits, and a pension plan that makes sense. *These are absolutely not the people for whom I am writing this book.*

Of course, if you decide that sycophancy is the smartest of all possible brand-building strategies, you might get lucky. You might become somebody's Igor, the operations guy who collects body parts for the mad scientist in charge of the organization. However, I'd put your chances of getting a job with any kind of power this way at less than one in a thousand. And this much is guaranteed: If you do get such a job, you are certain to be hated and reviled in it.

You are also certain not to work for very sensible people. Sycophants frequently add a bizarre note to the working life of executives that the intelligent ones don't appreciate. For example, there was the president of John Hancock who once casually mentioned to his meeting management people that he'd enjoyed the harp music at some event. For years afterward, at every event, there was a harp. Finally, the puzzled guy said to me, "David, what's with all the harps?"

The smartest bosses understand that sycophants are not just annoying; they are actually dangerous. They will, generally speaking, overuse what you say, do more than you ask, and use your power to cudgel everyone around them.

For example, I once said to a few of my employees, "I'm not sure I like the commission structure in this one area. I really think we should reexamine it."

The next thing I knew, there was a riot in the ranks of the sales force because their commissions had been cut.

> **Don't be a suck-up. Smart bosses know that sycophants are dangerous, because they overreact to anything the boss says.**

Of course, I didn't *say*, "Cut the commissions." I said, "I'm not sure they're right. Take a look at the situation." But in an effort to please me, these people went off and made a mess of things. A more useful kind of employee might even have come back to me and said, "We took a look at it, and we think you're wrong. The commissions are perfectly fair."

Do not develop a reputation for sycophancy. Do not allow yourself to be thought of as someone who is afraid to speak his or her mind. It will brand you as mediocre, and you will never rise as high as you want to.

THE CONTRARIANS: DON'T BE BITTER

Let's talk about the next personality type you don't want to be branded as: the contrarian.

Contrarians are equally as warped as the sycophants, but with the opposite effect. They always open their remarks by saying, "Let me be the devil's advocate here. . . ." They are the 10 percent of any organization's population who believe that the way to be true to themselves and to stand out from the crowd is to disagree with everything the boss has to say. In other words, they disagree for the sake of disagreeing.

The boss starts to cringe when these people come to his or her office, because it is an unpleasant experience every single time.

These people are not contrary because they happen to be feisty personalities who enjoy a good argument. No, they are contrary because they really despise the boss. If you are in any position of authority, they truly dislike you.

Why? In most cases, because they are the boss's intellectual superior. They are often better educated. And they cannot understand how the boss got this far. They wonder, "What happened to me?"

I will give them credit: They are fearless. But they are just as worthless as the sycophants are. First of all, you can pick up tidbits of information from contrarians, but it is not advice. Their assessment of any situation is too colored by their embittered outlook to actually be valuable.

Second, like the sycophants, they are dangerous in action. In fact, they are even more dangerous than the sycophants, who do what you don't want in an effort to please you. With contrarians, when you decide that you actually *do* want to do something, they spend all their time behind the scenes trying to unwind it.

Finally, contrarians tend to spend a lot of the company's benefits money on shrinks, hoping that someone will cure their incurable sense of frustration, and on doctors, because they are so constitutionally— as my grandmother would say—bound up. I prescribe milk of magnesia for the entire group.

I hope your sunny outlook puts you far outside this category of employee, because if you are branded as a contrarian, most bosses will devote considerable effort to figuring out how to get rid of you. But even less neurotic personalities can ruin their reputations by making the classic contrarian mistake: They assume that intellect trumps all other qualities in business.

> **Avoid the contrarian trap. Don't assume that your tremendous intellect alone is enough to propel you to the top. It isn't. You'll need the right kind of character, in addition to brains.**

The truth is, it's taken for granted that you are smart. Around eight million Americans have IQs over 130.

People with IQs of 135 or 140 are as common in organizational life as bad coffee. They're everywhere.

Your brains and your education entitle you to nothing more than a chance to succeed. You'll have to be thought of as *more than smart* if you want to actually get ahead. You'll have to demonstrate the right kind of character. You'll have to add to your brand the attributes of a third personality group: the balanced players.

THE BALANCED PERSONALITIES: NOT TOO HOT, NOT TOO COLD, THESE PEOPLE ARE JUST RIGHT

The balanced personalities—usually about 20 percent of the people in any organization—have the personal courage to tell the boss when he or she is right or wrong. They do it respectfully. Their opinion is based on the facts. It has merit. To an intelligent boss, those opinions are more valuable than gold. In healthy organizations, only the people with a reputation for balance rise to the top.

Usually, it takes time to become one of these people. You have to work for a lot of different styles of boss to figure out which ones are willing to listen to you and which ones are not. You have to watch the boss handle his or her own

> **Develop a reputation as a balanced player who is able to give advice that is worth trusting.**

boss to see how it's done, or to learn how not to do it. You also have to have worked long enough to develop a true conception of your own value and enough confidence in your opinions to push back when the boss is wrong.

There is also an art to giving advice, and you have to learn it.

One guy who once told me that I was dead wrong on an issue had yet to learn that art. I told him I disagreed with him and asked him why he felt I was wrong.

He went on to say that he was much smarter than I was on this particular subject, and he didn't care what I thought. Hmmm . . . let's review the leverage here.

I pointed out to him that it didn't matter how much smarter he was.

He said, "Why not?"

I said, "Because I have all the power."

Oh!

I had the power to say yes or no, and he had only the power to give advice. But his advice was no longer useful because the decision had already been made, and he had to learn to execute the decision in such a situation.

Timing is important. You have to figure out when it's appropriate to speak and when something is probably too far gone to be challenged. If you feel very strongly about something even after a decision is made, it is fine to say, "I disagree with you, but I'll certainly do as you've told me." You just have to make it clear that you respect the boss's right to make the final call.

> **Learn the art of giving advice. Do it before the decision is made, not after, when you will appear to be challenging the boss's authority.**

If, however, the boss's decision involves something illegal, you simply have to resist, even if it costs you your job. Otherwise, it may cost you your career down the road.

Troy Normand, for example, certainly paid a stiff price for failing to fight back hard enough against his bosses' bad judgment at WorldCom, where the biggest accounting fraud in history came to light in 2002. Normand was a member of WorldCom's finance staff. According to the minutes of a meeting released to congressional investigators, Normand said that he had questioned his superiors' accounting practices and considered resigning over them, but ultimately "did not communicate his concerns . . . because he was concerned for his job and has a family to support." This was definitely a deal with the devil: Normand wound up pleading guilty to fraud and conspiracy charges in October of 2002.

If your boss proposes something illegal, try reasoning with him or her. If reason doesn't work, go sideways, go upwards, blow the whistle, and call in the authorities. Just do not compromise your integrity for any boss. People will not care that you were only following orders when they decide never to trust you again.

Of course, balanced players develop strong personal brands not just because their advice is good, but also because they are not afraid to do the one thing that all good brands, from Oprah Winfrey to Coca-Cola, do: differentiate themselves from the competition. Balanced players are not afraid to go against the grain occasionally and stand out in stark contrast to the crowd.

Let me tell you about a moment some years ago when I decided to do something that was counterintuitive, to say the least. It had been a particularly good year, and I was offered $100,000 as a long-term bonus. The John Hancock board had already voted me the money, but I saw a real choice in front of me.

Was it better to be just one of the 20 people to whom the board had said, "Job well done," or was it better to be the one person who told the board, "Know what? Keep the money and give me something more valuable"?

I decided it was better to be unique. So I told the chairman that cash was not the currency I wanted. What I wanted was the ability to prove myself at a higher level.

The chairman was shocked, but my strategy worked. I wound up being given both the money and the wider responsibilities I had asked for.

Of course, balanced players are not unique because every single thing they do is unique. They don't stand out because every transaction

> **Don't be afraid to stand out from the crowd. It will help to brand you as a balanced player. But pick your moments carefully.**

stands out. That is rebellion for the sake of being rebellious, and it will brand you as a contrarian.

You will be branded as a balanced player only if you know how to pick your moments. You have to have a sense of when you must go with the flow or risk being viewed as self-destructive or disloyal by your boss, and when you can afford to do something different and be rewarded for it.

BOSSES WANT THEIR BRANDS POLISHED

The third thing that bosses want from you, after loyalty and good advice, is for you to polish their personal brands. They want you to make them successful and make them look smart, and sometimes, I will admit, that is a challenge.

But it is a challenge that has to be met, no matter how unappealing the boss is. Anyone who takes the attitude, "My job is not to make my boss look good, it's to make me look even better," is not long for this world.

Look at the contrast between two big personalities who served as White House chief of staff in the 1980s: John Sununu, the former New Hampshire governor who held the post under former President George Bush, and Jim Baker, who held the post under former President Ronald Reagan.

Michael Duffy of *Time* magazine described Sununu's style this way: He "ran the White House as if he were president." President George W. Bush's chief of staff, Andy Card, offered this take on Sununu: "He is the smartest politician ever—and he will tell you that." Asked which former chiefs of staff he admires, Card said, "Jim Baker served President Reagan extremely well."

In other words, Sununu thought the situation was all about him. And that is why he eventually got the gate. Baker, on the other hand, understood that his job was all about putting Ronald and Nancy Reagan in the right light. He was so clear about his duty to serve the boss's legend that he once said he did-

> **Understand that it's your job to polish the boss's reputation. Do not make yourself look good at the boss's expense.**

n't need to have a vision, "because the guy down the hall has one." And that is why he wound up with a promotion to secretary of the treasury.

As irksome as it may be, you have to give the spotlight to the boss. And you can only hope that the boss will be generous enough to share it.

Of course, one of the most valuable things you can do to make your boss successful is to compensate for his or her weaknesses. If the boss is brilliant but disorganized, the best way to win his or her gratitude and respect is to keep the trains running on time. If, on the other hand, the boss is dull-minded but methodical, the person who is able to offer a few good ideas is likely to be the most valuable to him or her.

> **Compensate for your boss's weaknesses to win his or her respect and gratitude.**

Finally, you probably also have to allow your boss to claim some of your work as his or her own. You may even have to put up with a particularly annoying sight—your boss behaving as if he or she is actually a highly creative person, now that he or she is armed with *your* ideas. This is not necessarily a bad thing. I actually consider myself fortunate in that I always had bosses who wanted creative ideas. They accepted my ideas, and in exchange they gave me a lot of leeway, both to be who I am and also to pursue interesting and important assignments that allowed me to build my own reputation.

> **All bosses will use you. The question is whether you are smart enough to use them to build a great reputation.**

The fact of the matter is, all bosses will use you. In their eyes, you are primarily an instrument to help them further their own careers. *The real question is whether or not you are smart enough to use them as well.* And what you want to use them for is to develop a reputation as someone who is destined for higher things.

If the relationship is simply that the boss uses you for your brains and accomplishments, and you get nothing in return but a paycheck, shame on you.

WHAT DO YOU WANT FROM A BOSS?

What do you want from a boss? Money? Perks? Head pats?

No.

What you really want, believe it or not, is to be trusted.

We've already talked about how much bosses long for loyalty, because loyal employees assuage their insecurities. You also should be looking for a loyalty-based relationship, even if it means sacrificing the great enjoyment of mocking the boss to your coworkers.

> **The two things you want from a boss:**
> - **Trust**
> - **A fair exchange**

This may be counterintuitive. You may think that if the boss is *not* asking you for loyalty, you are getting the same paycheck in return for a smaller investment. You are giving him or her the benefit of your brains, but not your soul.

But there are problems with such a completely clean, professional exchange. For one thing, you will get nothing beyond a paycheck in return. Organizations that value you only for your business skills—a lot of Wall Street firms fall into this category—are very antiseptic. They tend to be built on addictions, but not loyalties: addictions to the money, addictions to the process. They are a bit like galley ships. The overseers don't care about the relationship. They just want you to keep rowing.

This is fine when times are good, but if you should ever fail to handle the oar well, you are overboard. Such firms will have no compunction about firing you and even ruining your reputation, if it serves their purpose.

On the other hand, a boss who trusts you will give you opportunities that can change your life—not because you are necessarily qualified to do whatever big job the boss is dangling in front of you, but because the boss knows that you will do whatever you can to make him or her look good.

For example, when the management of John Hancock first asked me to run a business, I was as surprised as anybody. I had come to the company as its head of communications, and after three years and some successes, the company's president took me to lunch one day at Boston's Algonquin Club and asked me if I wanted to take charge of the group insurance business.

It was a little out of my line. I was a marketer; I'd never had an operations job in my life. But I like to try new things, so I agreed. We had a very pleasant lunch, and we were just getting to the club's famous macaroons when the company's president said, "Do you have any questions?"

I said, "I have one. What's the group business?"

My bosses at John Hancock were willing to give me an unlikely opportunity because they trusted me. And I understood the nature of the agreement. They were offering me a chance to be thought of as more than just a communications person. Thanks to their trust, I was able to build a reputation as someone who could bring home the bear—and without that reputation, I never would have had a shot at becoming CEO.

> **A boss who trusts you will give you opportunities that will allow you to be considered executive material.**

In return, I made them money. A lot of money.

The second thing you want from a boss is a fair exchange. If your boss is taking your ideas right and left and making tremendous demands on your time and energy, he or she had better be giving you something significant in return: decent compensation, public credit for your effort, and, most important, the kind of experience that will allow you to call the shots when you decide to leave him or her.

In fact, while monetary rewards are nice, the kind of deal that matters most early in your career is one that allows you to take on responsibilities that you otherwise couldn't, to work with clients you'd otherwise never get near, to build a personal brand, and to put the name of the firm—ideally, another attractive brand name—on your résumé. Your motto should be, "Give me respect now—I'll take the money later."

> **Early in your career, experience is more valuable than money.**

Ultimately, what you really want is a boss who actually allows you to learn something. Of course, there are many ways to teach: by intent, certainly, but also by example, by proximity, by osmosis, or even by negative example. As long as you are gathering some experience that will help you get ahead in the future, the bargain you make with even the most unpleasant boss may not be a bad one.

I have had at least 20 bosses in my career, and I must say that I've learned a lot from every one. I haven't liked all of them, for sure, but if nothing else, many of them taught me about problem personalities—something I wanted to learn about, so that when I saw one again, I'd know it. And because of the motley crew of bosses I've had, I did learn to recognize certain kinds of superiors and how to handle them.

The next chapter will offer advice for dealing with particular categories of bosses. Some bosses will do everything they can to stand in your way, and some will go out of their way to make sure that you shine.

PUT YOUR BOSS
ON THE COUCH

A s we said in the last chapter, what you want from your bosses is a good deal. In exchange for the things you do for them, you want them to help you build your brand.

Not all bosses, however, will give you that help. And it's not always immediately apparent which ones intend to stand in your way and which ones intend to give you a hand.

That is why it's important, particularly when you don't know a boss well, to put the boss on the couch and play amateur shrink. Be observant and take mental notes on his or her behavior, and you will soon have an inkling of the advantages and the dangers that this person poses for your brand.

It's an old cliché that there are only seven basic plots in all of literature. There are a similar number of basic plots in organizational life, too—a handful of core boss personalities whose profiles are worth recognizing. Of course, not every boss will fit into one of these categories. But many bosses will. And learning to recognize these types is valuable, because there is a good chance that the type of boss someone is will tell you what he or she is going to say about you.

THE LITTLE LEAGUE PARENT: DON'T STAY A CHILD TOO LONG

Because your bosses are generally older than you, many of them will treat you like an errant son or daughter. They may demand more than they should, as if you were family and you owed them an outrageous debt of gratitude for making you who you are.

Especially when you're young and new in your career, it's easy to fall for this line of argument, because you are not really well trained for organizational life. You have, however, spent the first 20 years of your life training in family dynamics. You know how to handle Mom and Dad, but you're not sure how to handle the boss. And you're completely susceptible to any boss who acts like Mom or Dad.

> **Parents are self-sacrificing. Bosses are not.**

"You're like a son to me," the boss says, and you believe him or her. Well, not quite.

While parents are famously self-sacrificing, bosses are famously not. It's very seldom that a boss will use his or her currency for you without getting something in exchange.

Even the greatest apparent generosity usually involves a return. For example, if the boss fights for you to be promoted, she invariably does it this way: She goes to her boss and says, "Look, I brought this guy in. He's really smart. He's done a great job. He's making us all look good."

In other words, the boss wants credit for having hired you and for having done a great job of rearing you. Whatever comes out of her mouth, here is what is really being expressed: "I am brilliant at developing talent. I want kudos upstairs."

Afterwards, the boss takes the elevator down to your floor and says, "I went up there and fought for you. If it weren't for me, you wouldn't have these opportunities." Translation? "I am the best manager anyone could possibly have. I want kudos downstairs, too." It may look as if the boss is fighting for you out of love. But in the end, the boss is doing it for herself.

If you need proof that your boss is really self-interested, just try bungling the job she recommended you for. Suddenly, not only is she no longer behaving like your mom, she does not even remember hiring you. As a matter of fact, she suddenly thinks they had

> **Understand that almost every nice thing your boss does for you is done not out of love, but to further his or her own brand.**

better check the file, because you are some kind of fraud who arrived on the company's doorstep wrapped in rags. She doesn't want her personal brand even *remotely* associated with yours. "I always suspected him; I never liked the guy" becomes the operative legend.

Of course, in business as in life, there are good parents and bad ones. The good parents, I prefer to call mentors. We'll talk about them next.

As for the bad parents, let's call them Little League Parents. They are just like the people you see shouting from the bleachers at their kids' sporting events because nothing's ever right. "I can't believe I put up with you," they say. "It's a good thing you have me, because if you didn't, you'd be out of here. . . . Do I have to save you again? . . . I'm reluctantly giving you this raise even though you don't deserve it." These bosses try to bind you by convincing you that you are inadequate.

Even *they* can be useful when you are a helpless infant. Since they like to think of themselves as extremely nurturing, Little League bosses may go out of their way to teach you a lot of very significant things. However, you can afford to have this kind of boss only when you're in your twenties and early thirties, because they will not allow you to develop a powerful brand in your own right.

You will get a mixed reputation out of them—praise, so long as no one gets the idea that you could function without the superior wisdom of Mom or Dad. "She did an okay job on that," is a typical comment. "I wouldn't give her too much more at the moment. Let me work with her and see if I can move her along."

The fact of the matter may be that you are fantastic. But this boss is sucking off your accomplishments by always emphasizing how much you need his or her help.

Under the Little League boss, you are not allowed to grow up. And if you do decide to leave the nest—no matter what you've done for him or her—you are, of course, an ingrate.

But it is just as likely that if you *don't* leave on your own, you will ultimately be thrown out. Inevitably, as you gain experience, you will start questioning Mom or Dad's judgment too much. Since this type of boss cannot bear the loss of authority, you become too expensive, psychically, to keep.

The truth is, there are no families in organizational life. And if your boss is the type who says, "We're family," skepticism is the only intelligent reaction.

Don't get me wrong. I'm not saying that people who work together do not grow close to one another. I'm just saying that family is a dangerous and inaccurate metaphor to use to describe that closeness.

The right metaphor is military. It is no accident that one of the best bosses I ever worked for, Bob Kleinert, had been a master sergeant in the U.S. Army.

THE MENTOR: HOPE FOR ONE OF THESE

The love and loyalty that develop between army buddies run famously deep. However, there is an important distinction between this brand of emotion and the familial brand: It is not extended to someone incompetent who might get you killed. Families have to embrace idiots. War buddies don't. The military relationship is all about mutual back watching for mutual benefit. Crises only help to deepen the relationship, because they allow you to prove to one another that, as a team, you can survive an onslaught.

> **Ideally, your boss is like a great platoon leader. You both gain strength by watching each other's back.**

Bob Kleinert was a genius at building this "Band of Brothers" feeling, despite being a famously tough boss. While I was working for him, I once did a fancy recruiting booklet for a sales meeting in Hawaii. At 2 a.m. the night before the meeting, he called me and told me I had to burn all the booklets. He was reading the brochure, and he saw that in one postage-stamp-sized picture, a man was wearing his pocket-handkerchief on the wrong side. The photograph had been flipped. This kind of imperfection was not acceptable to him. So, we spent an extra $540,000 to flip the picture over, reprint the booklet, and messenger the things back again.

On the other hand, he was not a fail-to-see-the-forest-for-the-trees kind of guy. And he built a real team. I started working for him in Connecticut, but he kept gaining more responsibility. When he was asked to come to the division's offices in Baltimore, he brought me with him, along with four or five other key people. And we fiercely protected his reputation. We would take bullets for him. If people at corporate headquarters were saying bad things about him, we'd be first in line to defend him. Most bosses, if someone says something negative about them, you shrug.

And we did our jobs with incredible zeal, just to make him look good. When we developed new products, we always said to ourselves, "This will really help Bob." It was personal, and we worked harder because it was personal.

How did Bob win that kind of loyalty from his subordinates? He earned it. Bob always took care of us. He made sure we were well paid. He made sure we had what we needed for our families. He gave us the benefit of his knowledge. Whenever he was promoted, he took us with him, rather than simply decamping at the first sign of greener pastures. He also made sure that our reputations rose in tandem with his.

> **A true mentor will make sure that your reputation rises in tandem with his or hers.**

Unfortunately, you'll never have a chance to work for Bob, because he died several years ago. But the kind of environment he created is the kind of environment in which you want to find yourself.

The key thing that mentors like Bob understand and the other types of bosses do not is that your brand has to change as you gain experience. Bosses of this type are not just good for you when you are in your organizational infancy. They help bring you through adolescence into adulthood, as well.

They start off by protecting you from the organization's predators and from the system itself. Then they move on to help you develop your skills. They help you build your brand with similar patience. They give you a little public praise, make sure your personnel file has strength in it, pass the word around the company that you are talented, and, basically, create for you an aura that says, "The boss likes this person, so he or she is someone to watch."

Mentors see to it that powerful people understand your accomplishments. And they use your successes to persuade their bosses that you should be given more responsibility.

Finally, when he or she believes you are ready for it, the mentor will work to move you up and out. And when it's time for you to leave the nest, whether you are leaving his or her department or leaving the company, the mentor will be happy for you. A real mentor is mature enough not to want to keep you forever. After a while, he or she needs fresh ideas, and you need fresh challenges.

> **A mentor understands that your brand has to change as you gain experience.**

It is never too early in your career to benefit from a mentor, and it is never too late, either. A boss like this will help you polish your brand whether you are 24 or 54.

THE WASTREL: PROPPING ONE UP CAN BE A GREAT EXPERIENCE

There are bosses whose self-image is all wrapped up in their taking care of you. And then there are bosses who expect you to do nothing but take care of them—mainly because they have made themselves helpless through neurosis or addiction.

That was true of one of my first bosses in public relations. I hadn't been working for him long before I figured out that I was working for an unusual person because he was not interested in doing a lick of work himself. And pretty soon after that I figured out why—all he really wanted to do was drink double vodkas on the rocks all day long.

Life with this guy was a constant series of misadventures. For example, he and I were once pitching the tourism business of a Central

American country. We had a meeting in New York City with the country's tourism ambassador and the umpteen people who worked for the tourism board of this relatively small nation. At lunch, my boss bragged that he sang opera.

Soon after, he and I traveled to Central America in order to continue pitching the account. One evening, a limo and a couple of army jeeps showed up at our hotel to take us to dinner, "for security reasons." We were whisked away to we did not know where, and we wound up at the presidential palace, where, much to our astonishment, we were served an incredibly elegant dinner with the president and his wife in an incredibly elegant room.

Afterwards, we were ushered into a parlor, and there was a pianist. It turned out that the president was an opera buff.

My boss accepted the president's invitation to sing, and soon there were murmurs of surprise in the room. He sounded just like Placido Domingo!

If Domingo had been a degenerate drunk from Long Island.

My boss *did* sing opera, just as he'd said at that first luncheon. What he had failed to mention, however, was that he sang weekend opera with some amateur group in the suburbs. Plus, he was, as usual, smashed.

God, it was embarrassing! Needless to say, we did not get the account.

One client we did manage to snag was the president of a third-world country. He was in America on a "goodwill mission," touring the country in luxurious style with a gigantic entourage. And he hired us to get him and his nation some good press, which we managed to do.

Then he went home and, before we had collected on our bill, was executed in a coup. My boss was under a lot of pressure from the higher-ups to get the money. So his idea was that I should get on an airplane, go to this country, and collect our fee.

I thought about it. It seemed to me that the guy who had executed our client was probably not going to be particularly eager to pay his predecessor's extravagant bills. I also suspected that he might have a short temper.

It took me months to talk my boss out of sending me, but I did talk him out of it—maybe because he knew that if I ever had an unfortunate encounter with a firing squad, he would have to go through the trouble of interviewing my replacement.

Though covering for this guy was not always pleasant, the truth was that he was a good boss in the important ways: He offered an excellent deal to somebody young, like me.

I had to do all his work and maintain appearances for him, but in return, I got to take on the assignments of a professional a generation older than I was, and I was introduced to powerful people that I'd never have met had my superior been clean and sober. It was, all in all, a terrific break, a great opportunity to build a substantial reputation early in my career.

> **Be tolerant of your boss's weaknesses, if those weaknesses yield opportunities for you to build your own brand.**

When you're young and new in your career, you may have to put up with a boss with some strange proclivities. But even a boss you don't particularly admire can be a good boss, as long as he or she gives you the opportunity to learn.

THE PARIAH: TRY TO KEEP YOUR BRAND DISTINCT FROM HIS OR HERS

Of course, you should not assume from my last story that all drunks are good bosses. Let me tell you about another big drinker I worked for, a maniacally undisciplined guy that we'll call the Pariah. Not only did he drink like a fish, but he must have weighed 250 pounds, and he smoked incessantly.

The Pariah was in a position of power; he was an executive vice president, a brilliant guy with brilliant organizational ideas. And he surrounded himself with brilliant people. I was surely the dumbest member of the team.

But even with all our combined cleverness, we couldn't make the Pariah look good because he was so outrageously impolitic. He'd be in the middle of a meeting with his peers, and instead of trying to maneuver his way around an issue, he would arrogantly intellectualize his way through it, and then end by telling the rest of the assembly that they were idiots.

He was so widely hated that the game on the executive floor was, how do we kill this guy? And his peers figured out that the way to destroy him was to keep his team of bright lights from accomplishing anything.

For us, this meant that if you had a systems project, you went to the back of the bus. Yours would be the last project that anyone would work on. Or, if you had an idea that needed capital, it would be voted down by the finance committee. Every time I came up with a marketing idea, someone would throw a flaming spear into it.

We were always ducking for cover. Everything we did was criticized by the rest of the company, and he never protected any of us in any way. Never. God, it was hard!

But eventually, his enemies' plan worked. Because he couldn't get anything done, he was blown out. And we were all left holding the bag.

The members of his team suffered one of two fates. Some members of the group thought that because they were loyal subordinates, any enemy of the Pariah's was an enemy of theirs. So, they chose to fight everyone else in the corporation at any cost. Of course, when Snow White was thrown out, the Seven Dwarfs were pitched into the village well.

But some of us survived, because, without betraying the boss, we had made it clear that we were loyal to the corporation, too.

For example, I had made alliances with other people at my boss's level and become someone that they could approach discreetly to send a message to him.

> **Try to form alliances outside your boss's circle in order to develop a reputation as someone who is loyal to the organization.**

The truth is, while you do owe your boss your loyalty, you do not want to be completely identified with him or her. If your boss is an appalling person, you certainly do not want to be seen as someone who simply does his or her bidding. Within an organization, the "just following orders" defense is generally no more successful than it was at Nuremberg.

Even when your boss is actively liked and admired, you do not want to appear to be his or her guy, someone who is owned by the boss. You want your brand to be that of someone who is useful to the whole organization.

You want this degree of self-sufficiency, first, because even the most popular boss can end up as a pariah, thanks to the soap opera of organizational politics.

It was at Citicorp in the early 1980s that the dangers of being completely identified with even a good boss became clear to me. There was a succession race under way for the CEO's job, with three executives openly competing for it. Now, Citicorp had a particularly ruthless culture. It was not only, "How can I steal your idea?" but, "How can I steal your idea, take credit for it, *and* kill you?" (A three-fer.)

A 1984 *Wall Street Journal* article captured the extra dose of ruthlessness that the succession race was adding to the place:

One former executive says rhetoric in the bank's upper ranks can sound almost feudal: an official tied to Mr. Reed, for instance, "is part of Reed's world," this former executive says. "If Reed is going to make it, so are you."

Well, eventually John Reed did make it and became the next CEO. But what about all those people who pledged their troth to the wrong lord?

I think their brands were in some trouble.

Merrill Lynch offers us another example: E. Stanley O'Neal had hardly been named president, COO, and heir presumptive to CEO David Komansky in 2001 before he replaced a number of senior executives described by the *New York Times* as "loyal to Mr. Komansky." Clearly, the new king had arrived, and the old king wasn't even off the throne before his retainers were executed. Machiavelli lives!

> **Try to be seen as a corporate-minded player, not the boss's lackey. Try to be a conduit between your boss and the rest of the organization.**

Aside from the danger of having to accompany your boss to the gallows, there is a second reason that you don't want your brand to be too closely identified with even the best boss: Even the most powerful king's courtier is never given the same respect as someone who controls the smallest duchy. The greatest respect goes to those who are both loyal to the regime and independent powers in their own right.

Ideally, you want to be seen as a conduit between your boss and the rest of the organization, an independent power who is universally trusted to convey information in all directions without betraying anyone.

It takes a lot of finesse to pull off this balancing act. But you'll have a much better brand if you are seen as someone who is able to move within the larger world of the corporation than you will have as the boss's lackey.

THE ONE-WAY USER: TURN AROUND AND TAKE ANOTHER ROUTE

Very few bosses mentor out of the kindness of their hearts. For example, why do I surround myself with the best people I can find and try to help their careers along?

So that I can work less. If those people stopped contributing, it would be a problem.

However, I also make sure that they are rewarded for that contribution. There is a big difference between a self-interested boss who offers you a decent exchange for your efforts and a self-interested boss who wants only to use you and forgets the exchange part.

It is this disregard for the things they owe their subordinates that makes a lot of very ambitious people bad bosses. For example, the social-climbing boss played by Sigourney Weaver in Mike Nichols' 1988 film *Working Girl* offers a classic portrait of a one-way user. She promises Tess, the working-class character played by Melanie Griffith, that she will help Tess escape the secretarial ghetto that she is unfairly trapped in. Then she steals Tess's ideas, gives her no credit for them, and tries to have her fired for pretending to be more than mere clerical help.

In his 1984 autobiography *Iacocca*, Lee Iacocca's portrait of Ford chairman Henry Ford II offers another example of a one-way user. Iacocca points out that Ford fired him after two of the best years in the company's history—and not without trying hard to ruin Iacocca's reputation first.

Why this treatment of someone who had made Ford a great deal of money and earned the company a lot of acclaim? Iacocca suggests that Ford's vanity was a key factor. Iacocca believed that he was getting too much applause in arenas that Ford wanted to keep for himself—Europe and Wall Street.

Iacocca recalls one meeting with Wall Street analysts and bankers in particular. According to Iacocca, Ford was tipsy, stood up, and "actually started to babble about how the company was unraveling." Iacocca took the floor after him in order to save face for the organization—an act, he says, that "may have been the beginning of the end for me." The next day, Ford dressed Iacocca down for "talking to too many people outside."

Vanity is a common thread among one-way users. They readily claim your accomplishments for themselves and use them to add to their glory. But no matter how extraordinary those accomplishments may be, one-way users don't think you deserve any particular recognition for them.

In fact, they will go out of their way to minimize your work and deny you the recognition you deserve, because they want to keep all the credit for themselves. If a boss like this has his or her way, your achievements will be a well-kept secret. Your efforts will do nothing at all to enhance your brand.

> Recognize the kind of boss who is a one-way user and who will do nothing to help you build your own brand, and then find a way to move on.

No one who is hoping to build a brilliant career can afford to work for a boss like this for very long. If you report to someone who is too selfish about his or her own brand to allow you to build *your* brand, it is time to move on.

THE WIMP: BRAVE ONLY WHEN IT COMES TO KILLING YOUR IDEAS

As with all insecure bosses, it is hard to polish your brand underneath a wimpy boss because he or she is probably too afraid of someone stealing you to praise you in public.

I once had a boss, for example, who was an incredible scaredy-cat. I did a tremendous amount of hand holding with this guy. I wrote all his memoranda, I wrote his reports, and I gave him every idea he ever had. Yet he never gave me credit for anything, and he was determined to hold me back.

However, the fact that this guy refused to talk me up was not the worst of it. The real trouble with Wimps is that they are too fearful to allow you to prove yourself in action. Wimps don't give you that opportunity because they are so loathe to make a decision.

You have to devote a tremendous amount of time to reassuring the Wimp that the memo for his or her signature that you've rewritten twelve times is all right, that the plan of action you have discussed fifty times is acceptable, and that the sky is not about to fall just because you have decided to actually do something.

And then this boss *still* solicits an infinite number of opinions before giving his or her okay to anything. The last person who was in the office—that's whose opinion the Wimp adopts as his or her own.

Some things really should be decided by committee. But there are a lot of things in organizational life that shouldn't be. Great new products, great advertising, and great marketing plans are usually the brainchild of one person—someone who feels that he or she has the freedom to propose something new.

Wimps will never give you that freedom because they are so terrified of saying yes to anything.

They are the classic organizational clog, a hardened artery in the body of the corporation. And if one of your ideas is ever given the chance to see the light of day, Wimps are not people you can depend on in the trenches.

The Wimp will say, "Okay, take that hill. I'll watch your back." But at the first sign of trouble, it's as if there's a trapdoor underneath his feet that leads to a bunker with a supply of canned goods. He disappears.

Wimp bosses do not allow you to build your brand because they don't allow you to do anything.

When it comes time to hand out the medals, however, the Wimp rewrites history and deludes himself into believing that he's Audie Murphy. The Wimp actually believes that *he* was the person who took the hill.

That's annoying. But what really counts for your brand is whether your boss actually allows you to *do* something. And this one will not.

THE KNOW-IT-ALL: HE OR SHE DOESN'T BELIEVE YOU *HAVE* IDEAS

I once had a boss who was never wrong. Let's call him "Jim."

Jim wanted some promotional kiosks placed around the corporate headquarters that would display slogans about synergy and other pleasant fictions. He wanted to be able to walk around, see the signs, and feel better about his life, as if we were all a big family and worked together as happily as the Seven Dwarfs.

The kiosks went up, and he came to my office *outraged*.

It didn't matter that there were other people in my office and we were having a meeting. He was just beside himself, because I had spelled "synergy" wrong on signs on 80 different floors and locations around the country.

He screamed at me, "You spelled the goddamned word wrong! I want those goddamned signs fixed today! Or it will be your job."

So, after he left, I went out looking for the nearest kiosk. The signs looked right to me. "Synergy" is, of course, one of those words that you are never supposed to spell wrong in corporate life because the higher-ups really believe in it. They don't understand that most of organizational life is the Hatfields and the McCoys, not "synergy."

I didn't see Jim until the very end of the day, when I knocked on his office door. I had brought the dictionary with me, a classic Webster's Second Edition with a red jacket.

He was still steaming. "Have you fixed those signs yet?" he asked.

I said, "No."

"Why not?"

"Because 'synergy' is spelled correctly." I had the page open to the word. I had the word highlighted.

He looked at it. And then he threw the dictionary into the wastepaper basket. "Your dictionary is wrong. Now, get out of my office."

He was never wrong. The Webster's was wrong, but not this guy.

Although not all of them are such screamers and many of them are better educated than Jim, he was definitely a member of the group called Know-It-All bosses.

These bosses never listen. In some ways, they are worse than the bosses who steal your ideas. The Know-It-All is generally not smart enough to steal your ideas, because he or she doesn't believe it is possible to have a better idea than his or hers.

And then when you go and implement whatever idea the Know-It-All had because you're loyal and you do the things you are supposed to do with a boss, if it fails, *you* get blamed for the bad implementation.

The Know-It-All cannot admit to being wrong, and that makes this type of boss dangerous. Know-It-Alls are always covering up behind themselves. The thinking goes this way: "I said I'd be able to do this, and after all, I am Superman. Since things went wrong, it must therefore be someone else's fault." This kind of boss may very well try to frame you for one of his or her crimes.

However, that is not the only threat he or she poses to your brand. The fact is, you will gain no meaningful experience from this boss. With some of the

> **Because the Know-It-All boss doesn't allow you to think for yourself, he or she has nothing to teach you.**

other, more dysfunctional characters you'll have as bosses, there is something to learn. But because the Know-It-All doesn't allow you to think for yourself, he or she has nothing to teach you.

Bad as the Know-It-All is as a boss, he or she is even worse as a subordinate. As a CEO, these types of people frighten me to death. They end up being so taken with their own misguided ideas and so incapable of listening to the people who work for them that they take down whole divisions. These are the people who end up taking down whole companies.

I try to avoid having this type anywhere near me. You should, too.

THE POWER BALANCE: YOU DON'T HAVE MUCH, BUT YOU DO HAVE SOME

We have talked a lot about the importance of understanding how much power a boss has over you, and how comparatively little power you have in return. But you are not powerless. And if you wield the power that you do have intelligently, you are on your way to building a great personal brand.

YOU CAN TURN DOWN PASSAGE ON THE TITANIC

The one time you have any control over which person you will be reporting to is when you are weighing job offers. Yet, too many people go into the interviewing process expecting just to be judged. You should be judging too, and considering whether the place and the potential boss will add to your brand—or whether they will squander your talents, brains, and efforts.

Many bad bosses will actually give themselves away during a job interview. A one-way user, for example, may not ask questions about the things you can do, but ask only about the ways he or she can use the things you do upstairs. A hypercritical boss may even start criticizing you. A hostile boss may be hostile before you're even hired. Is your potential boss sniping at his or her assistant in front of you? It's a good bet that if you take the job, he or she will soon be sniping at you, too.

Even if a potential boss does not set off any alarms during the interview process, it is smart to inquire about the reputations of the people for whom you'll be working. Not just the reputation of the company, but also the reputations of the people. Talk to current employees, ex-employees, and the reporters who cover the company for the media, and you'll get a good feeling both for the culture of the place and for the character of the person to whom you'll report.

If it doesn't seem to be a situation where your brand will grow, don't take the job.

> There are four types of power that you have against a boss who wants to stop you from building your brand:
> - The power to avoid an obvious disaster
> - The power to leave
> - The power to impress other powerful people
> - The power to someday influence the boss's reputation the way he or she once influenced yours

> Inquire about the reputation of a potential boss before you take the job. Don't sign on with someone who is unlikely to help you enhance your brand.

YOU CAN GET OUT OF DODGE

All relationships with bosses are a Faustian bargain. You want experience and contacts. They want hard work and performance, and maybe even your immortal soul.

The bargain is meaningful as long as you are learning. Even if your boss is a monster, the job may be worth the pain if it is truly broadening your horizons and allowing you to add substance to your personal brand. If, however, the boss is a monster and your horizons are as narrow as his or her mind, find a better job.

Where ambitious people tend to get a case of the stupids is by staying in a comfortable place long after they have already gained whatever knowledge and power they were going to gain.

That's why there are so many miserable people in their forties and fifties trying to figure out how they missed the curve. They missed the curve because they were lulled into mediocrity. Their brands were locked in place long ago.

> **Don't get too comfortable. If you are not learning and adding to your brand at your current job, leave.**

They always thought that there was going to be time to change jobs and prove themselves by doing something different and more challenging. And then they wake up one day, and they are working for someone 10 years younger.

When you stop learning from your boss and your experience and stop adding to your reputation, it is probably time to move on. And if the organization is not willing to move you up, it's time to move yourself out.

YOU CAN MAKE FRIENDS IN HIGH PLACES

If you are terrific at your job, yet you are being kept down by a bad boss, there is a good chance that somebody above that boss has noticed you. If, for example, the boss's boss asks a question in a meeting and your boss cannot give a thorough answer, but you can, that will tell your boss's boss a lot.

If you are getting signs of sympathy, gratitude, and interest from over your boss's head, it may be worth it to stick it out even with a miserable boss. At some point, your boss's boss will probably choose you over your superior. The one thing you have to be careful of in such a situation, however, is using your relationship with other powerful people to whine about your boss.

If you do that, not only will you appear untrustworthy for violating the chain of command, but you may also offend the executive's pride in his or her powers of observation. For example, if someone comes to me complaining about his or her boss and insults me by thinking that I cannot see what is going on, I will never, ever put that person on my staff.

Now, it's different if I say to him or her, "I'm concerned about this situation. Tell me about it off the record." In that case, frankness is in order.

If you are under the thumb of a bad boss, you should also know that there are times when the hierarchy is probably going to be strictly observed and times when it is likely to be shaken apart.

> **You may be saved from a bad boss by winning a good reputation among the higher-ups. But do not complain about your boss unless you are invited to do so.**

When everything is going well, everyone is congenial and even fools are allowed the illusion of power. It's when there is a crisis and things are going badly that people's true character is revealed, and it becomes clear who is running scared and who is running the show.

I learned that lesson when I was four years old, one afternoon in my grandfather's little grocery store in Utica, New York. I was always with my grandfather, who had become blind in his later years; I was his seeing-eye grandchild.

That afternoon, a man named George who used to forage for mushrooms for us had brought my grandfather a burlap sack with eight or ten live blackbirds in it. My grandfather had grown up in such a poor part of Italy that the villagers used to trap blackbirds for meat. And long after he could afford chicken, he never lost his taste for blackbirds.

My grandmother had gone upstairs to get a bite to eat, so my grandfather left the sack of birds in a corner.

Well, one of the blackbirds pecked a hole in the sack, and they all got out and were heading toward the store's open door. I said to him, "Grandpa, Grandpa! The blackbirds got out."

And my grandfather got very upset. So, in Italian, he said, "Close the door, close the door!"

He had a cane. He decided I was going to spot them for him, and he was going to kill the blackbirds. So I started shouting, "There's one there! There's one here!" And my blind grandfather started swinging his cane.

Soon, there was lettuce flying and cream of wheat being knocked off the shelves. Bins of coffee were falling, and Ovaltine was being sprayed over the floor. I don't think he got within three feet of a blackbird, but he was swinging his cane wildly. It was like a one-man food fight. And I was jumping around, all excited. I was four years old. It was action to me.

Eventually, my grandmother heard this commotion and came trundling down the back stairs.

Then she started yelling, "Open the door! Let them out!" And my grandfather kept saying obediently, "Yes, Magdalena, yes, Magdalena," in Italian.

My eyes widened. Up until that moment, I had thought my grandfather was absolutely in charge of everything. Since people did what he said, I thought he was the boss. I suddenly realized who the real boss was.

My grandmother usually let him believe that he was in charge. But this was a crisis, and she had showed her hand.

That's what happens in a crisis. People show their hands. So if you are suffering under incompetent management, you should welcome a little upheaval. It will let you measure the true power of your boss—it may be more limited than you think. It will also let you learn who are the real powers in your organization, the people you need to win over if you are to rise.

> **Do your best to shine during a crisis, and you may escape a bad boss.**

And times of upheaval will let powerful people learn what you can do, too. Do your best to shine whenever there is a sense of emergency in your organization. Crises allow the people in charge to separate the wheat from the chaff—and, hopefully, to separate you from a bad boss.

YOU CAN ENJOY A DISH BEST SERVED COLD

A pleasant story from my career: In 1975, I got a call from a headhunter who said that Ingalls, one of the big Boston advertising firms, was looking for someone to head up its public relations arm. So, I traveled to Boston from Baltimore, where I was working, and I interviewed with a guy named Joe Hoffman, the agency president. He asked me back again. I met a few clients, Joe Hoffman offered me the job, and I accepted.

I told my wife we were moving. I told my boss I was leaving. I was about to go to Boston to look for a new home, when something strange happened: I never heard from Joe Hoffman again.

I called Joe Hoffman. He didn't return my call. I called him again. He never called me back. I called the headhunter. She wouldn't return her calls, either. Clearly, he did not want to get caught paying her fee.

I spent a few weeks in a state of panic. I'd quit my job, and they were already looking for somebody new. But Joe Hoffman never called me back, and no explanation was forthcoming.

Fortunately, I'd been frank with my boss about what I was doing. So, I told him that my new job was falling through and asked if he would keep me on. Thankfully, he agreed.

Ten years later, I was named vice president of communications for John Hancock. We were doing an advertising agency search, and Ingalls was one of the top three finalists.

I hadn't met with any of the advertising agency people myself—my staff had. At the time, John Hancock was the only prestigious account in the city of Boston that was up for grabs, so all the advertising agencies were climbing over one another to get our business.

I tried to avoid social events where I'd be the recipient of any kissing up, but I did happen to wind up at a cocktail party with the people from Ingalls, including Joe Hoffman.

We were introduced. Joe Hoffman did not remember me at all. But he clearly wanted this account so badly he could taste it. He wanted to take me to lunch; he thought we should do this and that together. He was prattling on and on about the wonderful future we would have together as best buddies.

Finally I said, "You know, we've met."

"We have?"

"Yeah, you offered me a job once."

He said, "Really. What ever happened?"

"You offered me the job and then never called me."

He said that was impossible.

"Oh, no?" I said, and started rattling off the names of the headhunter, the people I'd met in his office, the clients he'd introduced me to. And then I explained that he had almost put me on welfare.

His eyes got larger and larger as the true horror of the situation became clear to him. Suddenly, his brand and his livelihood were in my hands, just as mine had once been in his.

> **Eventually, you may have as much power over a former boss's brand as he or she once had over yours.**

Was I going to allow him to add a prestigious client to his résumé? Or was I going to tell my secretary not to put his calls through?

I did neither. He did not get the account, but I did allow him to go through the whole excruciating process of competing for it.

When you are suffering under a bad boss, just keep this cheerful thought in mind: The tables may turn. The truth will out. The skunk will someday reveal itself. And you may very well wind up in a position of power over the person who once abused his or her power over you.

When you finally do become one of the elders of the tribe, life can be sweet, indeed.

LEARN WHICH ONE IS
THE PICKLE FORK

In this chapter, we'll talk, believe it or not, about etiquette—about developing a style of behavior that will enhance your personal brand, not destroy it. We will concentrate on the handful of rules that, in my experience, are most essential. They will range from the obvious—don't dunk your tie in the soup—to the far less obvious—don't bring your dates to company events, even if they are invited.

But let's start with a more basic question. This is an informal world, and most people pride themselves on not being stiff. Why does etiquette even rate?

For the answer, let's turn to an expert, Judith Martin—a/k/a Miss Manners—who constantly wrestles in her work with the question of whether manners even have any meaning in the modern world. In an essay entitled "The Case against Etiquette" in her book *Miss Manners*

Rescues Civilization, she hints at two theories of manners, both of which are worth our consideration.

First of all, she says that the most serious charge she hears against etiquette these days is, "It's artificial! It's elitist! It's old-fashioned! . . . And—*it uses forks!*"

In other words, a lot of people think that etiquette is merely about knowing which piece of silver to use at a formal dinner when there are a dozen weird-looking implements in front of you. Pickle-fork etiquette is clearly elitist, a way in which people prove that they are members of the right club—and differentiate themselves from the members of the wrong club.

Miss Manners *detests* this use of etiquette as a class identifier. In her view, manners "require compassion and respect." They are a way of making life nicer for your fellow man, not of elevating yourself above him.

Let's face facts: Miss Manners is an idealist. The truth is, both theories of etiquette apply in business, and both help to explain why good manners are an essential tool of brand building.

First of all, you had better have good manners because without them, you will seem to be clueless about the world that successful professionals inhabit—definitely not a candidate for membership in the club. And whether it's fair or not, people will interpret your cluelessness about how to behave as a sign that you are clueless about how to do your job, as well.

For example, in Lee Iacocca's 1984 autobiography *Iacocca*, he tells the story of how his predecessor as presi-

> **Good manners are essential to a good personal brand for two reasons:**
> - **They will show that you belong in the world of senior executives.**
> - **They will demonstrate your compassion and respect for the people around you, a quality that good leaders must have.**

dent of Ford Motor Company met his fate at the hands of Chairman Henry Ford:

> I wish I could say that Bunkie got fired because he ruined the Mustang or because his ideas were all wrong. But the actual reason for the firing was nothing like that. Bunkie Knudsen was fired because he used to walk into Henry's office without knocking. That's right—without knocking!

Bad manners identified the guy as someone the chairman did not want to have around.

Second, you'd also better have good manners as a way of showing your compassion and respect for your bosses, colleagues, and subordinates. This is one of those qualities that will identify you as a leader and that intelligent bosses will look for when considering whom to promote.

FIRST, TRY NOT TO EMBARRASS YOURSELF

While the first rule for doctors is, "Above all, do no harm," the first rule for brand builders is, "Above all, avoid embarrassing yourself."

Reputations are usually shaped by patterns of behavior. However, sometimes a single embarrassment can be enough to alter people's opinion of you forever—particularly if that embarrassment seems to bring things you have only hinted at before into focus, or if it seems to reveal the hypocrisy of the reputation you've established in the past, or if it is all that people know about you because you have not yet established yourself, or if it is especially memorable.

It is smart, therefore, to go out of your way not to associate your personal brand with anything unethical, unsa-

> Sometimes a single embarrassment is enough to alter people's opinion of you forever.

vory, or just plain ugly, even if the action seems like a good idea at the time.

For example, I was once working for a company at a time when there was a terrible drought. Public officials were telling people not to water their lawns and not to run their washers during peak-use hours and were setting up fines for people who wasted water.

So my boss, a senior vice president, came up with his own water conservation program, thinking that this would make him seem like a really progressive guy. He took me and the puzzled head of administration into the men's room and explained, "We have to tell people that for a number two, you flush every time. But for a number one, you flush every *other* time."

I was there because he wanted me to write the memorandum. The administration guy, he had literally draining a toilet to see how much water it used as compared to the urinal. And the best part was, we had to debate how you know, when you're looking in the urinal, whether it's been used or not—in other words, whether to flush or to wait.

"Well," my boss said sagely, "if it's been used, it's more yellow."

I offered, "Would you like me to put that in the memo?"

"Absolutely," he said.

So I wrote this crazy memo. Fortunately for me, he was self-important enough to insist that it go out under his signature, and it became the joke of the year at my company.

In fact, my boss made the entire situation as ridiculous as possible. He even sent his poor VP of administration into the men's room with a clipboard to make sure everyone was following policy. You'd be standing at the urinal, and it was an "After you, my dear Alphonse" situation, in which you'd have to negotiate with the guy next to you to decide who would go first and who would go second.

Thankfully, we soon had rain, and another corporate crisis was averted. But my boss never lived down his reputation as the flush-control guy. Here is what did him in: He might have been a senior vice president, but he revealed the level that he really should have been working at—bathroom monitor. Suddenly, everyone understood who he was. His limitations came into sharp focus, and his career went nowhere.

You never know when the world will decide that one bad move represents you. So be very, very cautious about associating your brand with anything that will make the world recoil.

> **Be cautious about associating your brand with anything that will make the world recoil.**

This is the most obvious of all possible rules. But it's amazing how many people ignore it.

DON'T WASH YOUR FACE WITH A PANCAKE

Personal habits in food and dress count for much more in business than most people are willing to admit. If you want success at a high level, it's important that you both look the part and act it.

Of course, looking the part is very difficult when you are young and badly paid. When I first went to work in New York City right out of college, I had long hair, I wore bell-bottoms, I didn't own a suit. I was from "upstate." What did I know about fashion?

Suddenly, I was thrust into the business world, so I went to a warehouse sale at Barneys, at the time one of the biggest men's clothiers in New York City. Of course, the warehouse sale included everything Barneys couldn't sell at a normal price—or even at a 25 percent discount. In the dank light of the warehouse, I saw a dark maroon-colored suit. I knew you were supposed to have dark suits for business, so I bought it.

I'll never forget the first day I wore it. I was on my way to work, heading into the building and feeling sharp. The head of the entire firm was entering, too, and as he got into the elevator with me, he said, with a puzzled look on his face, "Have you been shopping at Brooks Brothers?"

It turned out that in the sunshine, my dark maroon suit was red. Not Santa Claus red, but red enough. Only two kinds of people can get away with a red suit: preppie golfers and clowns. I was neither, but I continued wearing it.

Finally, an older guy named Dolf took me aside and told me what even my boss wouldn't tell me. "I've been watching you," he said. "You're a very smart young guy. But a person in a red suit has no credibility." He made me see that no one would take me seriously until I started dressing more professionally.

> **If you want to be taken seriously, dress professionally.**

Of course, dressing professionally does not mean that you have to be a cookie-cutter copy of everyone else in your profession. As long as it falls within the bounds of respectability, an individual style can make you seem more confident than your peers. Insurance executives, for example, tend to be a very gray bunch, but I happen to like bright ties, and I've always worn them at John Hancock (with dark blue—not maroon—suits).

After I became CEO, I noticed that the ties around the office became brighter. After I'm gone, they'll probably go back to being dull.

Here is the point: There is a huge difference between wearing a red suit because you don't know any better and wearing bright ties because you do. One is an informed choice, and the other is a screamingly obvious product of ignorance. People will respect an individualist, but not an ignoramus.

> **An individual style is fine, so long as it is not the product of ignorance.**

There is no question that in some situations, a mildly contrarian fashion choice will give you a strategic advantage over the competition. Consider, for example, David Boies, arguably the most admired lawyer in America since his devastating deposition of Bill Gatcs in the Justice Department's antitrust case against Microsoft, in which he made Gates appear to be a petulant liar.

Boies is rich and famous, but he dresses like a high-school math teacher, ordering his cheap suits and ties by the dozen from the Lands' End catalog.

This unpretentious look enhances his style of argument, which is all about clarity, not unnecessary flourishes. His modest style helps reinforce the message, "All you are getting from me is unadorned common sense." In other words, cheap clothes are part of what makes the Boies brand so persuasive.

The first rule of dress in business is, above all, dress appropriately. Make sure your clothes are the right size. Make sure they won't make the people around you nervous. Then, if you are confident enough of your own grasp of the situation, dress for strategic advantage. Dress to define your brand. Whatever you do, think about what you are doing when you get dressed in the morning. It matters.

It's also important to make sure that your table manners indicate that you are a worldly person, one who is familiar with the rules of civilized life.

> **Make sure your table manners suggest some familiarity with the rules of civilized life.**

I've seen plenty of tuna-fish-spraying executives who eventually were fired because no one could stand to be near them. But the saddest case I've ever seen of eating habits doing someone in involved a beautiful young woman whose table I sat next to at the Shun Lee Dynasty restaurant in New York City.

I was waiting for someone for lunch, and the tables were so close together that you couldn't help overhearing the conversation at the next one. After a few minutes, I realized that a job interview was taking place.

The beautiful young woman was being interviewed by two older men. She sounded as if she came from the Midwest, but she appeared as polished as any New York City native. She looked great; she had on a great outfit; it seemed as if things were going well.

When it came time to order, she urged the older men to order for the table, since they knew the place well. In other words, she was smart enough to conceal her lack of familiarity with Chinese food.

So their lunch was brought. One of the dishes was moo shu chicken. She was offered a steaming pancake and picked it up with a smile. And then, much to the astonishment of her tablemates and the waiter, she slapped it on her face, where it broke into little pieces.

She had mistaken the pancake for a washcloth. This one impulsive move accelerated lunch considerably. It established her as someone the two men were no longer interested in having lunch with, let alone considering for a job.

Manners that demonstrate a lack of knowledge will hold you back. The people who could benefit your career won't trust you. They'll assume that your lack of knowledge carries over into fields that are important to their business, as well.

So, if you're going to find yourself at working dinners with a dozen pieces of silver in front of you, take the time to learn which one is the pickle fork. It might not seem relevant to your personal brand. Trust me, it is.

MAKING ASSUMPTIONS ABOUT PEOPLE YOU DON'T KNOW CAN BE FATAL

While it's smart to turn yourself into a book that can be easily judged by its attractive cover, it is to your advantage to be very cautious about judging other people the same way.

Since I rose to a position of power at John Hancock at a relatively young age, I frequently found myself snubbed in meetings with outsiders who assumed, incorrectly, that some gray-haired Hancock person was the one who was making the decision. And, inevitably, I made these people suffer for their presumption.

> **Be cautious about judging other people too quickly on the basis of their appearance.**

One of the most outrageous examples of this occurred surprisingly recently, when I was CEO of John Hancock, but not yet chairman. John Hancock was doing business with a consulting firm, and its chairman asked to meet with us. It was intended to be nothing more than a half-hour of friendly chitchat with two of his people—a distinguished-looking gray-haired guy and a considerably younger guy—and me.

Unfortunately, the chairman of this consulting group was very confused. He kept referring to the gray-haired guy as Steve, even though his name was Bill. He talked to "Steve" at length about the time they'd played golf together. And he ignored me, the client, completely.

All the rest of us were puzzled and uncomfortable until finally, after about 20 minutes, I got it. He thought Bill was Steve *Brown*, then chairman of John Hancock. And I was no one worth bothering with.

The question for his employees was whether or not to correct him. The less senior guy finally did the right thing. He pointed to Bill and said, "Mr. Chairman, this is one of our employees. And this is David D'Alessandro, the CEO of John Hancock."

The chairman was stunned. He'd made himself look like a complete phony, and an out-of-touch phony at that. Not only did he not have the faintest memory of someone he'd spent an afternoon playing golf with, he also didn't know one of his own senior employees. He'd embarrassed Bill, slighted the client, and created a story that will live on in infamy.

Take a lesson from this guy. Do not hurt your reputation by deciding too quickly who deserves your attention and who doesn't. Snobbery will only trip you up.

> **Don't be a snob. It's dangerous to slight someone you don't know.**

Of course, I've seen people make even stupider assumptions. I worked at one place where one of the top executives was gay. One of my peers, oblivious to this open fact, started venting in a meeting with this executive about how the company should not be promoting homosexuals. Needless to say, thankfully, the guy never went anywhere in that company.

> **Don't be a bigot. People will find you idiotic.**

My advice is, keep your prejudices, whatever they are, to yourself. And if that seems impossible, at least know your audience before you flaunt your limited intelligence.

I actually learned not to judge people too quickly very early in my career. When I was in the PR agency business, we were always working at a frenetic pace. One morning I decided to bring in a temp to do some typing for me for a presentation that I was giving that very day.

The temp was late. Finally, I saw a young woman wandering around aimlessly, so I handed her a sheaf of notes and said, "Hi. All this needs to be typed now. We have a presentation at noon."

She complied pleasantly, while I hovered unpleasantly over her shoulder.

The next day, the big boss from Chicago came into the office and introduced everyone to his daughter Anne. Sure enough, Anne was my typist, except that she was not a typist at all. She had just been taking an informal tour of the place when she'd been abruptly corralled by me.

> **Don't make assumptions about people you don't know. Slow down and observe them first.**

She was a good sport about the whole thing and never told her dad. And she taught me something valuable—to slow down when it comes to other people and to observe them for a while before assuming that I know who they are.

Not only is this a kinder, gentler, more humble way to deal with the rest of humanity, but it also may keep you from developing a reputation as a horse's ass.

WORK WITH COCKTAIL DRESSES AND ALCOHOL IS STILL WORK

The most dangerous of all work occasions for your career are the ones that are supposed to be fun—the office parties, the victory celebrations, the conventions in another city, the off-site meetings designed to build morale.

Consider, for example, the case of six Barclays Capital investment bankers who went out in London one night in 2002 to celebrate closing a deal. They drank some of the rarest wines in the restaurant's cellars and spent $62,000 on dinner. The restaurant promptly bragged about the check to the press, and newspapers all over the world proclaimed this the most expensive meal per capita in history.

The end result? Even though the bankers had paid for the dinner out of their own pockets, Barclays soon fired all but the newest member of the group. Though Barclays refused publicly to tie the firings to the dinner, reportedly the bank was not happy to have its employees setting a record for excess in the middle of an economic downturn.

Fine wine is one thing to do yourself in for. Shrimp is another. Yet, I almost got killed once in a shrimp stampede. I was with a bunch of sales guys and their spouses at a convention, when the hotel pulled out these big bowls of shrimp. People reacted as if the hotel had served up bowls of gold coins instead. They were stuffing shrimp into plastic bags that were lining their suit pockets. Funny, not one of the shrimp stuffers was ever promoted by me.

You have to be aware that you are being judged even in circumstances that seem like recreation. Unfortunately, a lot of people, when offered *any* temptation—food, alcohol, sex, an opportunity to speak frankly—in a work-related situation succumb so completely that they destroy their reputations in the process.

People tend to treat office parties like snowstorms, a moment in time when everything freezes and nothing counts. They think it's a timeout: "We can do anything we want right now, and there won't be any memory of this tomorrow."

> **Beware of company events that are supposed to be fun. Even if it seems like recreation, you are being judged.**

Well, guess what? Everyone does remember. As far as your reputation is concerned, if the event is in any way related to work, it is work. It's all work. The fact that there are cocktail dresses and alcohol there simply means that the situation is a tougher test of your character.

So, not only should you not let your hair down at a social event sponsored by the office, but you should be twice as cautious about protecting your personal brand—or you'll feel very bad in the morning.

I have a basic rule about office parties: Don't drink. It is also not smart to try to use these events to impress the higher-ups.

> **Don't drink at office parties. And try to avoid your boss.**

Though people will tell you the opposite, I am convinced that nothing good can come of spending more than five minutes with your boss at a cocktail party. First of all, if you spend more than five minutes with your boss, you look like a suck-up. And if you spend more than five minutes with your boss and you have a drink in your hand, chances are, you are going to say something you shouldn't say. The smartest strategy is to say hello and move on. There are plenty of real suck-ups who will occupy a boss's time. Even four hours on the golf course with your boss is as dangerous as it is helpful. Choose your conversational topics carefully.

Of course, the most dangerous of all work-related occasions, one that is best avoided altogether, is the infamous off-site meeting.

I've been to some off-site meetings that were a day long and some that were two weeks long. I've been to some where I've been locked in a windowless conference room with no air conditioning, chairs that didn't roll, and yesterday's Danish. And some where I have been flown to a luxurious hotel in a tropical paradise.

I've been to some that were nothing but a long, stiff show-and-tell about what each division or department was doing. And some that offered a kind of hip corporate spiritualism about having the right karma and working together, where the only things missing were campfires and holding hands and singing Kumbaya.

The accommodations and the agendas do not matter. They are all snake pits for reputations.

They are always driven by some executive's need to bring the organizational "family" together and to feel as proud as a mother hen of his or her brood. Well, organizational families are always dysfunctional. When they are thrust together in a strange place with a group of people they don't know all that well, the temptation for the "children" is to regress completely into a state of pure id. Somebody *always* drinks too much

> **Try to avoid off-site meetings. They are snake pits for reputations.**

and commits some form of self-immolation or other. And if an office affair isn't already going on, there's a good chance that a dozen of them will be happening by the time you get back from the off-site.

My favorite of all the off-sites I've been to was a dreary session at some camp in the middle of nowhere in the Catskills. We had these outside "training" consultants—the real snake-oil salesmen of the business world—in theory to get the team to communicate better. It was a kind of mental Outward Bound, endless "catch me if I fall" kind of stuff that was supposed to build camaraderie. And we did these videotaped exercises in which we had to interact with one another, then play the tapes back for the other people in our group to analyze.

Well, early one morning we were all sitting there half-awake, eyelids half-closed, half-dead with boredom, reviewing yesterday's sessions, when one interaction took a surprising twist. There, up on the screen, were two of the people in that very room making love.

Apparently, the couple had sneaked into the classroom at night, done the deed on the conference table, and *thought* they'd erased the tape. They were very inventive, but it was still very bad form.

I'll tell you, that was some attention-getter. And for all intents and purposes, the careers of those two were destroyed. No one ever took them seriously again.

If you are unlucky enough to work for people who like off-site meetings, just make sure that you are extremely skeptical of the advance press for these junkets. The executives organizing them will tell you that they are all about relaxing and bonding. Maybe they'll even hire consultants who will tell you the same thing.

Actually, they are the *worst* possible occasions for relaxation. If you don't want to add a whole string of unsavory descriptives to your personal brand—drunk, floozy, glutton, loose lips—do not let your guard down for a minute.

KEEP YOUR MYSTERY

In business, you are now allowed a private life that is actually private, which even 20 or 30 years ago you were not. Back then, you could not rise to the top of a corporation if you were divorced. An office romance could kill your career. And you certainly couldn't go anywhere in business if anyone discovered you were gay.

Fortunately, we have grown up a lot as a society. No one is going to go on a witch-hunt these days to learn the real truth about your sex life.

We now reserve that kind of intolerance for politicians, whose careers really can still be derailed by the "wrong" affair.

Of course, there are still some things that are not good for your career—for example, getting arrested. But generally, your personal life is your own—until you decide to make it public. Then you must be prepared to take the consequences for your brand.

If you date ridiculous people who like to chew gum during their meals, fine. Just don't bring them to corporate events. If you do, do not expect your colleagues to adjust to your standards. They won't. They will judge you harshly for the company you keep.

In fact, they will judge you harshly even if you introduce them to the best-looking, most intelligent, and most charming people in the world. When I was single, I almost never took a woman to a company event. There are all kinds of dangers for your brand in making your dating life public. If you show up with too many different dates, you are a "player." If you show up with too many good-looking dates, you are a "real player." And people will worry that you are not quite stable enough to be entrusted with a big job.

But if you always show up with the same date, that's dangerous, too. If you break up with the person after everyone gets to know and like him or her, you will be branded as either a harpy or a cad. And your career may actually suffer.

You will be judged most harshly of all if the person you are dating happens to be someone you work with. Of course, it would be complete foolishness to say, "Don't date anyone in your organization." People in offices date.

> **Do not take your dates to company events, even when they are invited, or you will be judged by the outcome of every romance.**

They have affairs. That's what happens when human beings are in close proximity to one another. But it is generally smart to keep it under wraps.

I worked with one guy, for example, who was really dumb. He was openly seeing the president's secretary. He broke up with her and broke her heart. She was miserable for months, and that meant she made the boss's life miserable, too—missing his calls, being unable to keep track of his schedule, etc., etc.

Did the boss blame her? No, he blamed the guy, who soon found himself transferred to another building in another city. Ah, chivalry is not dead.

UNDERSTAND THAT MARRIAGE, UNLIKE DATING, IS A PUBLIC INSTITUTION

It's important that you understand the fundamental difference between marriage and dating. If you are only dating someone unsuitable, discretion will save your reputation. But if you marry someone unsuitable, keeping the spouse out of the office won't work. Marriage is a public institution, and how, why, and whom you marry inevitably colors your professional brand.

Some years ago, as I was about to get married for the second time, one John Hancock director took me aside and gave me some advice. "You are forgiven one divorce," he said. "You married too early, you grew apart, you spent too much time on your career. But if you blow the second marriage, it's about *you*." And he made it clear that the reputations of many-time losers definitely suffer.

Harsh, but true, as the case of Stephen Hilbert suggests. Hilbert was the founder of the beleaguered insurer Conseco who resigned under pressure in 2000. At last count, Hilbert has been married six times—the sixth time to an exotic dancer in her early twenties. Unfortunately, this colorful home life may have hastened his end, since it seemed to confirm suspicions that his vows—whether business-related or marital—could not be taken too seriously. No wonder the *Wall Street*

Journal called him "the Rodney Dangerfield of the insurance world."

> **Marriage is a public institution. It will color your brand.**

And whatever you do, do not allow your spouse to speak for you. It's extremely common to find your spouse harboring the hostility and resentment for your boss that you yourself cannot afford to dwell on—so common, in fact, that the *Wall Street Journal* ran a column in 2002 titled "Help! My Spouse Hates My Boss."

Do all you can to discourage your better half from nursing this dislike. While there is a vicarious thrill in watching your spouse light into a difficult boss, do not give in to this temptation. I've been on the receiving end of spousal hostility, and let me assure you, it has never done anything for anyone's career.

Once, at a convention, I agreed to meet one of my employees and his wife for a drink. I found them in the bar. He was a skinny little guy, and he was perched on the arm of a loveseat that his wife, who was enormous, filled to overflowing. They were absolutely Jack Sprat who could eat no fat and the wife who could eat no lean.

We had barely said hello before Mrs. Sprat lit into me, angrily accusing me of diminishing her husband's role and failing to appreciate his many gifts. A spouse who flies off the handle is bad enough, but what was worse was the fact that Jack did nothing to try to control her. In fact, I could tell that he was *gleeful* that his wife was telling me off.

I was younger then, so I decided to engage her. Now, I'd just give both of them a Medusa look and, hopefully, turn them to stone. But I said, very sympathetically, "Mrs. Sprat, you're right about your husband. He's an extremely intelligent guy. But let's admit what we both know about him. He's lazy, and he doesn't get things done on time."

This little bit of sympathy disarmed her completely. "You're right," she said. "It's impossible to get him to clean the gutters." Suddenly, we were friends. And I spent the next half-hour listening to her complain about him and nodding in agreement.

The next day, Jack showed up with a black eye and said plaintively, "What did you do? My wife is taking your side now."

What were the chances that I had any residual respect for the guy at this point? With one passive-aggressive move, he managed to ruin both his professional reputation and his domestic bliss.

Do not use your spouse as a stand-in to make the complaints you yourself are unwilling to make or to lobby for a raise or promotion for you. It will give you a reputation for weakness that you cannot possibly live down.

> **Do not allow your spouse to lobby the boss for you or to complain to the boss. It will give you a reputation for weakness.**

On the other hand, make sure that you *do* consider the boss's spouse a stand-in for the boss. And talk to the spouse as respectfully as if you were talking to the boss.

There is nothing more stupid than being so preoccupied with impressing a senior executive that you bulldoze over his wife or her husband. Yet I see it all the time at cocktail parties: younger people sucking up to someone in senior management while ignoring his or her spouse. And only slightly less stupid is fawning over the spouse in such an obsequious manner that it pisses off both halves of the couple.

My advice is, treat the husbands and wives of the higher-ups like human beings. It's not just the decent thing to do, it's the smart thing to do as well. Because if the spouses do not like you, it is only a matter of time before your brand is poisoned.

> **Treat the husbands and wives of higher-ups like human beings, or they will make it their business to poison your brand.**

My personal experience of spouses in a business setting is that they are all Sicilian in temperament: They understand instinctively that revenge is a dish best served cold. So, they wait until the right opportunity presents itself. Let's say a guy named William offends your wife at a cocktail party. She may not tell you about it. But eighteen months later, when you go home to her and say, "I've got this promotion to give out," William is eviscerated before the lights are out.

She says, "That Peter guy is very personable. William, I'm not sure about. I think he might turn off a lot of clients." And the decision is made. William's brand is now fixed in your mind: He has a difficult personality.

Of course, while it is smart to get the boss's spouse to like you, you don't necessarily want to be *liked*. Once, there was this guy with Nero-like power over me. It was thumbs up or thumbs down, and if it was thumbs down, off with my head.

He had a very pleasant wife who was substantially younger than he was, around my age, and we hit it off. We wound up having a lot of laughs at one cocktail party, and the big boss came up to me afterward.

"My wife really likes you," he said.

"I like her, too," I said. "You're a lucky man."

I was single, and he asked me if I had a girlfriend. I told him no.

Then he said coolly, "Well, my wife's not available."

I was completely taken aback. I may not have been the smartest guy in the world, but I was not dumb enough to hit on the boss's wife.

But clearly, Nero considered even friendly conversation to be out of bounds. I don't think I said a word to his wife again for the next few years. In fact, I carried a crucifix around and soaked myself in garlic juice just to keep her at bay if it ever occurred to her to say another word to me.

Be sure to be kind and polite to the boss's spouse. But it's dangerous to actually think you are friends. The conflicting loyalties may prove bad for your career.

> **Be kind to the boss's spouse, but don't get too involved. The conflicting loyalties may be bad for your career.**

PATIENCE IS A VIRTUE, MAYBE EVEN *THE* VIRTUE

In this chapter, we discussed the basic rules of business etiquette that I see people break most frequently, with the worst results. However, I have by no means given you a comprehensive guide to organizational manners. If you live long enough in the vertical village, you are guaranteed to find yourself in many bizarre and puzzling situations that no book will have even grazed.

It's important that you arm yourself with an understanding of what constitutes good manners in the most general sense, so that you can maintain your poise, no matter what your job throws at you.

Manners are about compassion and respect, as Miss Manners says; so when in doubt, try to be a decent human being.

Manners are also about knowledge, so try to learn the rules of good sportsmanship for every work-related activity.

Finally, manners are also about patience.

The people who develop the best personal brands in organizational life tend to be impatient for results, but very patient in the way they handle the people and situations around them.

> **Manners are about**
> - **Compassion and respect**
> - **Knowledge**
> - **Patience**

They try to understand the concerns of their colleagues before yammering on about their own concerns. They forgo an opportunity to impress the boss in order to make his or her spouse feel at home. They give up that second drink in order to maintain their self-control. They keep that affair secret even when it might be much more fun to flaunt it.

The essence of good business manners is the ability to stand back, take a deep breath, and decide what is the right thing to do or say—

even when everyone else in the room is diving into one form of instant gratification or another.

So, take a moment to do the kind, polite, discreet, dignified thing whenever you can, and you will probably be considered extraordinary by the people who will be judging you. Smart leaders understand what good manners *really* mean: You possess the self-discipline necessary to become a leader yourself.

KENNY ROGERS IS RIGHT

So far, we have spent a lot of time talking about how crucial it is for you to seize opportunities to build your brand. If you intend to have a big career, however, it is also important that you pick your battles and avoid spending your time and energy on efforts that will never move your brand forward.

There are some situations in which you have lost the contest to build your brand before you even step onto the field. The smartest thing to do in such cases may be to give up trying to impress people, cut your losses, and look for opportunities someplace else. Yet, too frequently, ambitious people refuse to recognize when their brand-building efforts have become an exercise in futility, and it is time to move on.

In "The Gambler," Kenny Rogers sang, "You got to know when to hold 'em, know when to fold 'em."

Kenny's right. You do got to know those things. In this chapter, we'll talk about when to fold 'em and when to run—not walk—away.

NEPOTISM MEANS "NOT YOU"

As I mentioned earlier, I grew up over the little grocery store my grandparents owned in Utica, New York. They were hard-working immigrants who had a brilliant son, my father, who became a college professor. Unfortunately, he also became a degenerate gambler, and eventually he lost the store, our home, and everything my grandparents had built on the horses. So my childhood definitely had its school-of-hard-knocks element, and people like to call me a "Horatio Alger" story.

They will often say to me, "Aren't you glad you had the upbringing you did?"

My response is always the same: What, are you kidding me? I would much rather have had my last name be Hancock. I would gladly have left a lot of life's painful lessons on the floor.

The best brand attribute you can possibly have in business is one that you have to be born with: the right last name. Ford, Rockefeller, Vanderbilt, du Pont, to name a few.

> **The best brand attribute you can possibly have in business is the right last name.**

This is true at your average family-owned car dealership, and it can even be true at large public companies, 60 percent of which, according to the Family Firm Institute, are family-controlled. It is true everywhere that the bosses or the owners have dynastic ambitions. If you have the right last name and a limited amount of intrafamily competition, your chances of rising to the top are excellent.

For example, did anyone believe that Bill Ford, who took over as CEO of Ford Motor Company in 2002, was the best of all possible executives to run the company in the wake of Jacques Nasser? Let's give Bill Ford credit. He was smart; he was talented; he was something that was very refreshing for the auto industry—an environmentalist. But, as many business journalists pointed out, his management experience was limited. Was he really the best possible person for the job?

The truth is, he didn't have to be. The Ford family, which still controlled 40 percent of the stock in Ford Motor Company, obviously wanted him there.

What happens, however, if you are missing this particular brand attribute, as Jacques Nasser was at Ford? In that case, you may well put in 30 years at the company, as Nasser did, only to find your ascension to CEO marred by an awkward power-sharing arrangement with the favored son, and then to be booted after a few short years when the son is ready to take over himself.

Even if you rise to the top of a family-controlled company, you can carry a big title without ever really being seen by the family as someone who should be in charge. You may be a placeholder more than a leader. And it is not just CEOs and would-be CEOs who find their ambitions frustrated at family-controlled companies, but also anyone who is competing with a family member anywhere along the line.

Unfortunately, at a family-run business, it is very easy to fool yourself into believing that you can succeed on merit alone. Maybe the patriarch or the matriarch treats you with a lot of warmth, and you start to think of yourself as one of the family. Well, the streets are littered with the corpses of young executives who thought they were as good as a child.

It's important to understand the mindset you are up against with dynastically inclined bosses. In his biography of Nelson Rockefeller, *The Imperial Rockefeller*, Joseph Persico tells a fascinating story from Rockefeller's time as governor of New York that illustrates this mindset perfectly.

Persico, who was a speechwriter for Rockefeller, was in a meeting at Kykuit, Rockefeller's home, to go over a draft of the governor's budget message with budget director T. Norman Hurd. It didn't matter that Hurd was a Ph.D. and a "leading authority on public finance." Rockefeller allowed his three-year-old son Mark to continuously interrupt him: "As Dr. Hurd started to speak again, Mark began talking. Nelson stopped to listen, not to Dr. Hurd, but to Mark."

Persico concludes, "Nelson Rockefeller was passing along an unspoken lesson absorbed from his own father—'These people work for us. Never mind their age, their position, they defer to you.'"

Family business owners don't have to be Rockefellers to think this way. So, if you are second banana to the father or mother, prepare to be second banana to the child. It does not matter how brilliant you are, or how important you are to the organization. Get used to being nice to that kid whose birthday party or graduation you just attended, because he or she will soon be your boss.

Even if the kid demonstrates no interest in or aptitude for the business, the chances are that somewhere down the road he or she will realize the irresistible advantages of starting a career as the designated heir. This certainly happened at a firm I used to work for. The founder's son had just graduated from high school, and I remember going to a party and hearing him dis his father's business mercilessly. He was going to Harvard, and he wanted nothing to do with such an undistinguished line of work. Needless to say, he is now president of the firm. And as for everyone else who had hoped to run that organization, they did nothing but keep the fire lit until the prodigal son came home.

Families do not build businesses in order to pass them on to anyone but family. At a family-run company, if you don't have the right last name, your brand will always be deficient. It will be the brand of a caretaker, a respected

> At a family-run business, if you don't have the right last name, your brand will always be deficient. It will never be the brand of a true leader.

retainer, a valued house servant, but never, ever the brand of a true leader.

Even if you *marry* into the family, your brand will probably still be deficient. You are likely to be competing with your spouse's brothers and sisters, who will inevitably see you as an interloper. And you cannot drink enough ouzos with the in-laws to change that.

Families can be remarkably cold about the distinction between those who do and those who do not share DNA with them. One consultant to family businesses recommends that they develop "creeds" that spell out things like voting control and stock ownership. He uses as a positive example one creed that sounds as if it is discussing eligibility rules for the Westminster Dog Show, not a business: "Only bloodline family members and their bloodline descendants may own stock in the company or vote." And God knows, even if you are allowed a voice in the company as an in-law, you had better not even think about getting divorced if you hope to keep your career intact.

> **If you marry into a family-run business, do not even think about getting divorced.**

The final drawback to being an outsider of whatever stripe in a family-run company is the danger of having your career injured by shrapnel. As family businesses pass through the generations and the number of potential heirs increases exponentially, so do the resentments about who deserves what. All the ancient questions about who pulled whose hair, who didn't do the chores, and who dropped the toy chest lid on whose hand get played out through the business. According to the Family Firm Institute, only 30 percent of family-owned businesses survive into the second generation, and only 12 percent make it into the third. Many dissolve into family feuds.

You may very well find yourself choosing sides among siblings whether or not you want to and derailing your career by making the wrong choice.

My advice is, learn all you can at family-run companies; but when the time is right for you to lead, find another sandbox to play in.

IF A GANG CONTROLS THE TURF, SET UP SHOP ELSEWHERE

Once, when I was leaving a company called Commercial Credit and choosing among job offers, I got a terrific piece of advice from one of the senior managers. I was trying to decide whether to take a job with John Hancock or to take a big job with Commercial Credit's parent corporation, Control Data, at its headquarters in Minneapolis.

Even though I had not been particularly close with this guy, he was willing to be slightly disloyal to set me straight. "Let me tell you something," he said. "You will never have an upward career in Minneapolis because the company is run by a Scandinavian tong." He used the word for a Chinese gang.

He went on, "The tong does not *like* anyone but Midwesterners of Scandinavian origin. It will never let you in. If you want a big career, you must be in an environment that welcomes diversity, where at least you have a chance."

That conversation is the primary reason I wound up coming to John Hancock. I took a look at the people on the top floors at John Hancock, and I found the opposite of what you'd expect in a conservative old Boston financial organization. The leadership was fairly diverse: two Jews, one Brahmin, two Irishmen, and a Midwesterner. I knew I could rise there.

Of course, that was in the mid-1980s. You might think that since then, all the exclusionary gangs that once discriminated on the basis of race, ethnicity, religion, sex, or sexual orientation have been routed out by better laws and a more sophisticated populace. Not so. There are still places where you are likely to bang your head against the ceiling simply by virtue of who you are.

Wall Street is a terrific example. Even at this late date, a powerful tong of Neanderthals makes it a difficult place for women to build a professional brand. By now, the "boom boom room" culture of the brokerages and trading floors, in which women are forced to deal with swinish behavior from their coworkers, is famous. But what is more apropos to this book is whether women are blocked from promotion and kept from putting together brands that spell leadership.

The federal Equal Employment Opportunity Commission seems to think so. In 2001, it filed a sex-discrimination suit against Morgan Stanley, estimating that as many as a hundred women might have been unfairly passed over for higher pay and promotions just within a single division since 1995.

And it's questionable how fast Wall Street is changing. Consider, for example, Smith Barney, whose Garden City, Long Island, office was the home of the basement party room called the "boom boom room" that gave a class-action sexual harassment and discrimination suit against the firm its nickname. In late 1997, in order to settle the "boom boom room" case, the company agreed to spend $15 million on diversity programs. By 2002, it was bragging that it had increased the number of women sales managers and assistant sales managers to 35 out of 349, up from just 11 in 1998.

That is still merely 10 percent. Let's hope that Smith Barney's first woman CEO, Sallie Krawcheck, who got the job late in 2002, picks up the pace.

There are many elements of your brand that you cannot do anything about—they simply come with the territory. Maybe you're adopted, or you went to a community college instead of an Ivy League school, or you are a single mom, or you were born in France.

If you want to build a big career, you cannot afford to waste years in a place where the power structure is going to be resistant to your brand, no matter what your performance. Chances are, you will never rise as high in a gang-run organization, although there is always the possibility that you will be the pioneer who breaks the tong's stranglehold. Of course, in the case of Wall Street, the compensation is so high that for some women the gamble is undoubtedly worthwhile.

However, it is important to be realistic. In an organization where the leadership is prejudiced against your kind, you will expend a lot of energy trying to break through the brick wall of their bias—the same energy that in another organization could have been spent acquiring fame, power, and money in a wide-open field.

> **Do not waste years in a place where the power structure is resistant to your brand simply by virtue of who you are.**

Be sure you make the decision to work in a place with this kind of prejudice with your eyes open.

DON'T LET THE HAZING GO ON TOO LONG

Let's talk about another place where people routinely lose perspective on their chances of building a strong, independent brand, and that is in established partnerships such as law firms, consulting firms, accounting firms, and architecture firms.

The basic dynamic of these places is that the old take advantage of the young. They hire the best and the brightest right out of prestigious schools. They may pay these people well, but they force them to grind away 14 hours a day, six days a week for years, generating big bills for the firm's clients, at work that may be well beneath their abilities, under conditions that can be cold, unfriendly, and demeaning—all on the off chance of making partner.

The young are willing to put up with this exploitation, not just because they want the money that comes with being made partner, but also because they crave the legitimacy and acceptance that partner status represents.

Partnerships take full advantage of that psychology. They are a lot like college fraternities, in that they are able to convince the freshmen to do all kinds of humiliating and self-destructive things because they want so badly to be a member of the club.

In fact, working for a partnership is the longest hazing on record.

It certainly sounds as if life as an associate at the law firm Clifford Chance in 2002, for example, resembled nothing so much as day after day of running the gauntlet naked with your underwear on your head. After coming in dead last for associate satisfaction among the 132 law firms surveyed in 2002 by *American Lawyer*, Clifford Chance asked six of its associates to write a memo explaining why the associates so disliked the firm.

The memo cited many, many sources of unhappiness among the associates, including a draconian billable hours requirement, unfairness in the way the assignments that would determine the associates' chances of making partner were doled out, and a general disdain for the associates on the part of the partners. Comments included, "The partners 'hate' the associates." One associate mentioned being yelled at and told, "We own you," by a partner.

The kick-the-dog syndrome is familiar. Over the years, I have seen thousands of young MBAs, JDs, and CPAs chase unpleasant old men who often are not anywhere near as smart as they are. And the old men's attitude is, "Look, I put up with the hazing, my grandfather put up with it, now you're going to put up with it. And I don't care if your father *is* a member of my club. I don't want to see you at my club dinner."

Of course, there are a few things to be said for putting in time at a partnership. First, even if you opt out before making partner, having the name McKinsey & Company, Pei Cobb Freed & Partners, or Cravath, Swaine & Moore on a résumé will add a certain star quality to your brand.

Second, since these places often attract very prestigious clients with a wide range of requirements, you may learn a great, great deal there.

Where smart young people go wrong is that they become addicted to the hazing, addicted to the firm. They focus so intently upon becoming partner that they become irrational about their chances. By some estimates, only 2 to 3 percent of new hires at public accounting firms ever advance to partner. The chances are just as slim at some law firms. At Cravath, Swaine & Moore, for example, there were 293 associates in early 2002, and a grand total of just six associates who had made partner in the previous three years.

> **At a partnership, do not become so addicted to the place that you are irrational about your chances of making partner.**

It is important to understand that existing partners are reluctant to make *anyone* partner. And if they are hostile to associates, it is because all those associates seeking partnerships are asking them to give up part of their equity.

They are not going to share that equity with you unless it is very likely that you will enlarge the pot by bringing in new business. Partnerships respect hunters above all. Unfortunately, many smart young people do not have it in their nature to hunt. Many of them are analytical types who prefer to skin.

> **If you are not a hunter, you will not make partner. So do not stay if the experience is not adding to your brand.**

If you are a skinner, face facts: It is not likely that you will make partner. So try to avoid the trap so many people fall into: They stay too long chasing something that will never materialize, long past the point where the experience will add anything to their personal brands.

In fact, as you move into your mid-thirties without making partner, not only does your brand stop growing, but it actually begins to look tainted to your employer. You begin to seem expensive and difficult. By now, you have more than paid your dues, you are likely to have a family, and you may be far less eager to get on that 8 p.m. shuttle flight to Topeka or Cleveland to hold a client's hand.

The partners start to think that they can buy what they want cheaper and younger. They are a lot like the successful middle-aged man looking for a second wife. People believe that the reason that middle-aged men often look for trophy wives in their twenties has to do with looks. Actually, it is because young women are so much more pliable, wide-eyed, and worshiping.

Partnerships, too, prefer pliable, wide-eyed, and worshiping.

"Well, excuse me," the partners start to think, "we're paying this person $200,000 a year plus a bonus, he doesn't make that much rain, and he is whining about the travel and the hours. Well, you know what? We can go to Stanford or NYU and buy two new graduates who are just as smart—and far more cooperative—for the same price."

Needless to say, it is not the best thing for your professional brand to spend 10 or 15 years in short pants, only to be abruptly fired.

> **Put yourself on probation. If you are passed over for partner twice, leave.**

To build a professional brand that will thrive whether you make partner or not, you need to be disciplined about the chase. If the situation arises where people who came in at the same time you did are becoming partners and you are not, put yourself on probation. If it happens again the next year, get out.

If you are passed over twice, it is time to find a better opportunity someplace else.

IF YOU'RE TALENTED, EXPECT TO HAVE YOUR DESK SET ON FIRE

There is no shortage of narcissists among the upper ranks in organizational life. But entrepreneurs are a special case: They are the narcissists' narcissists.

They usually have all the good qualities of narcissism in excess: a charismatic personality, an ability to see the big picture and innovate, and a gift for inspiring their followers. And they have all the bad qualities in excess, too. Anthropologist and psychologist Michael Maccoby sums up the problems of narcissistic leaders this way:

> Of all the personality types, narcissists run the greatest risk of isolating themselves at the moment of success. And because of their independence and aggressiveness, they are constantly looking out for enemies, sometimes degenerating into paranoia when they are under extreme stress.

Obviously, it's hard to remain in favor with someone who is "constantly looking out for enemies," and it's hard to become an independent power underneath a paranoiac. So entrepreneurial ventures represent a special danger for someone who is hoping to build a powerful professional brand.

> **Entrepreneur-run companies are dangerous for anyone who is hoping to build a powerful professional brand.**

Yes, you can learn a tremendous amount from these cowboys. But it is generally not smart to stay too long with most of them for a few reasons.

First, with entrepreneurs, everything is personal. Everything is a reflection on them. So they will virtually always try to put you in an "owe-me" position. They may give you an extra three weeks off when you need it.

They may bring you a turkey on Christmas. They may lend you the money to buy a house. But it is not something you have earned, and it is not free. It is a favor that is designed to bind you.

And in their eyes, any independence or sense of deservingness on your part equals betrayal. So you will almost always betray them in the end.

Silvio, the guy who owned the shoe-repair shop in New York City where I used to have my shoes fixed, is a perfect example. Silvio had a cobbler working for him who had been with him for 50 years. The man was now 81 and ill, and he wanted to retire.

> **Four reasons it's hard to build a brand under an entrepreneur:**
> 1. Everything is personal, and any show of independence is a betrayal.
> 2. Entrepreneurs are insanely controlling.
> 3. They don't like to share.
> 4. They like to play Toy Soldier with their employees.

He could hardly hammer on a heel anymore. Did Silvio understand?

No. He felt used. "Ah," he told me, "he's leaving me, after all I've done for him!" Silvio would not have been happy unless the guy had died polishing a pair of wing tips.

With an entrepreneur, the only alternative to betrayal is slavery. At many entrepreneurial ventures, the employees are actually worshipful of their brilliant, idiosyncratic masters and mistresses and will do anything for them, including limiting the development of their own careers. Not smart. Do not allow yourself to be bound by gratitude or charisma to the point where your brand cannot grow.

Second, entrepreneurs are insanely controlling. The best of them are benevolent despots. The worst are crackpots. In fact, their habit of getting their way actually encourages them to develop manias and to impose those manias on the people who work for them.

For example, I had a client once who took his finicky aesthetic ideas to insane extremes. He had his lobby redesigned in high 1970s modernism, with a white receptionist's module that looked like an eggshell. He got off the elevator one day and looked at his receptionist, a white woman. He said, "I'm sure you are very good at what you do, but you're the wrong color. You don't look good in the eggshell."

So he fired her and hired a black woman for visual contrast.

I worked for another entrepreneur who was equally finicky in a different direction. He saw the employees of our firm eating at their desks one day and thought it was appalling.

So he issued a directive: No eating at the desk. Of course, we also had a separate directive: If you're not with a client, no going out to lunch. So, in effect, we were prohibited from eating at all.

The guy didn't relent until I shamed him by organizing an "under the desk" movement. We stopped eating *at* our desks and started eating underneath them.

If the entrepreneur wants to control the look of the office, or the way you dress, or the kind of food in the company cafeteria—as many of them do—you can bet that he or she wants to control the way you do business. If you work for an entrepreneur, prepare to do things his or her way.

Entrepreneurs do not like to share. It is their land, and you are just a serf who works it. In the best case, you will get to keep what you've raised. But when you go to ask if you can buy the land, you generally have a problem.

Entrepreneurs are often stingy with the equity in their company. Even if they are generous enough to give you an ownership stake, they are almost guaranteed not to want to share some things that are even more important to the brand builder: credit for the company's successes and any degree of control.

Entrepreneurs are successful precisely because they believe they are always the smartest one in the room, crucial to all decisions. If you

demonstrate any ability to make decisions without them, watch out. Often,
the worst thing you can do in their eyes
is to be truly good at your job.

> **Often the worst thing you can do in an entrepreneur's eyes is to be good at your job.**

John H. Patterson, the entrepreneur who founded the National Cash
Register Company in 1884 and set the gold standard for autocratic
behavior, had a simple motto: "When a man gets indispensable, let's
fire him."

He also had what *Smithsonian Magazine*'s Mark Bernstein calls
"an absolute genius for firing people." One executive discovered that
he was out when he came to work one day and found his office furni-
ture on the NCR front lawn—in flames.

Among the people whose strength irked Patterson was Thomas J.
Watson, who went on to found IBM in the wake of his canning. Even
today, strength is still a firing offense at many entrepreneurial firms.

Remember, whatever power you gather at an entrepreneurial company is not really yours. It can be withdrawn at any time at the whim
of the king.

*Finally, entrepreneurs are subject to the "toy soldier" syndrome
with the people who come to work for them.* They are the business
equivalent of the spoiled kid who goes to FAO Schwarz and wants the
biggest, brightest toy soldier in the window. He gets the soldier, takes
it home, and plays with it for a while. Then he breaks its legs and aban-
dons it in the corner.

And given the paranoid streak of many entrepreneurs, it may not
be enough just to fire you once you are not so shiny anymore and you
have worn out your welcome. Instead, you may have to be pulverized.
Your commissions may be withheld, your reputation may be attacked,
or you may be sued—none of which will add luster to your brand.

It is much smarter to hit the door before you provoke this degree
of vindictiveness. Entrepreneurial companies are terrific places to

> **Entrepreneur-run companies are not good places to become a leader in your own right.**

gather experience, up to the point where you are ready to become a power in your own right. Then you are better off finding a place that does not resemble an absolute monarchy in which to build your own brand.

Building a big career requires a lot of discipline. You may very well find yourself working for an organization where it is structurally impossible for you to rise any further.

You may be frustrated, or you may be comfortable, even happy, there. But the one thing you should not do is stay.

When the way forward is blocked, for whatever reason, gather your courage and go. If your brand is being stifled, it is time to pick up your cards and find another game.

IT'S ALWAYS
SHOW TIME

I t is the nature of storytelling to favor what is dramatic and ignore what is not. And it's safe to say that most of the stories in this book so far have dealt with Big Events—moments of victory, tragedy, or breathtaking stupidity that decide a career.

But I don't want to give you the wrong idea. Reputations are *not* usually made by Big Events. They can be undone by a Big Event—the wrong scandal can kill you—but they are rarely made by one big positive move.

Sure, that fantastic presentation you gave that landed a big client may open up your bosses' eyes to your potential. It may even win you a promotion. But before the promotion is a week old, the basic attitude of most bosses is, "What have you done for me lately?"

For the most part, it is not the single Big Event that defines you, but the patterns that you establish, brick by brick, over time. It is your day-to-day behavior in a business setting that gives your brand its shape—how you deal with people, how you make decisions, what your work habits are, what you seem to be good at, and what you seem to be bad at. And no matter what transaction you think is occurring during your workday, and no matter how trivial or boring it seems, there is always another transaction taking place that is about *you* and the impression you are making.

> **Reputations are usually built brick by brick by your day-to-day behavior.**

Unfortunately for their careers, most people pay very little attention to the way they handle the mundane stuff. They have the mistaken idea that the only thing that matters is landing the client, not being pleasant to the boss's assistant on some ordinary morning.

This explains why there is such a tremendous disconnect between the reputations that people assume they are building and the ones they actually do build. People think that their coworkers and bosses are keeping score only on Game Day, not on practice days. Meanwhile, they are constantly on display, the scoreboard is always active, and they can dig themselves such a hole that even a spectacular performance on Game Day won't make up for it.

> **You are always on display. When it comes to your brand, there is no such thing as a transaction that doesn't count.**

I learned this lesson the hard way as a young manager. Fifteen years ago, I commissioned an anonymous poll in which my direct reports were asked what they thought of me.

When I got the poll results back, I was stunned. As a boss, I considered myself tough but fair, corporate-minded but empathetic. Yet clearly, my day-to-day demeanor had made a very different impression. People said that I didn't listen well. That I almost always thought I was right. That I discounted ideas other than my own.

Well, I don't consider popularity important, but I think fairness and openness are vital, because you cannot run a successful business without intelligent dissent. The last thing I wanted was a reputation for being incapable of listening to the people who worked for me. From then on, I tried to align my day-to-day behavior with the values I considered important and the brand I hoped to create. I'm certainly not perfcct now, but I am much more the kind of manager I want to be.

And I never would have become a CEO if I hadn't changed. The truth is, the importance of the way you handle yourself every day only increases as you move up in an organization. The pyramid narrows, there are fewer and fewer slots for promotion, and the competition for them becomes fiercer and fiercer. Little things matter even more, because your bosses are looking for ways to distinguish between you and your equally smart and accomplished peers.

> As you rise and the competition for promotion grows stiffer, little things matter even more.

It's the same in any highly competitive endeavor. When a movie actor, for example, is vying for a role against a hundred other actors, he or she has already met the prerequisites of type. That's a given. Then it becomes the little things that set the actor apart. The producer says, "You know, I like the way that person walks into the room." And that is what decides who gets the part.

In business, your walk is not likely to be the deciding factor, but a degree of grace in the way you behave at moments you consider unimportant very well might be.

The truth is, no moment is unimportant. With everything you do, you are constantly adding to and subtracting from your brand, so it's smart to be conscious of the impression you make every day.

As a counterweight to all the Big Event stories in this book, let's look at the brand dilemmas posed by all the small events on one very ordinary day.

IT'S 6:30 A.M.: DO YOU KNOW WHAT SKIRT TO WEAR?

You wake up at 6:00 a.m. on a Tuesday. You've now had a lot of Tuesdays in your working life, no big deal. You shower, and you think about your schedule for the day.

Are you meeting a client? Are you meeting your boss? Are you making a presentation? Are you going to the airport? Are you going out to lunch?

These questions lead to a bunch of others as you decide what to wear. Will you be taken more seriously if you wear a suit? Or will you be seen as a stiff?

If you're a 5'10" woman and you are meeting with a 5'6" man, do you want to wear heels or flats? You don't want him to feel short—or maybe you do.

Which perfume? Which cologne? How much?

The fact is, two dozen decisions loom every morning before you have your pants or skirt on. And if you are not making them consciously and strategically, you are a fool.

> **You will make two dozen decisions before you even have your pants or skirt on in the morning. Make them consciously.**

This seems obvious, but it apparently is not, since so many people make such bad choices. For example, I once went to a presentation made by a woman who, it was well known, had actually been a former Miss America contestant. This may be a great brand attribute in certain situations, but not necessarily when you are giving a business speech. Nonetheless, this was the attribute she chose to flaunt.

The fact that she was now 40 pounds heavier than she had been in her pageant days did not stop her from dressing as if she were still 22 and walking down a runway. Confirming the impression made by her outfit was the fact that when she presented, she strutted. Hand on the hip, turn, drop the shoulder. It was hilariously inappropriate.

All the women in the room immediately hated her. The men enjoyed the show, but no one took her seriously. She actually had some substance that was worth listening to, but she made it impossible for people to listen.

You, however, are smart enough, while you rifle through your closet, to calibrate the way you dress to your day.

7:45 A.M.: THE FRIENDLY GUY AND OTHER IRRITATIONS

You have only just arrived at the train station, and it's already show time. In the waiting room, you casually meet a lawyer whom you don't ordinarily see, but whose firm your organization occasionally does business with. He slows you down with friendly chitchat, and you wind up not having time to buy a cup of coffee before the train arrives.

You don't really want to continue the conversation, but he sits next to you on the train anyway. For the next 20 minutes, he asks what is happening at your company and what is happening with your work and the kids, deftly intermixing personal and business questions.

In other words, he will not allow you to read your newspaper in peace. You have a few choices here. Do you let your irritation show?

Maybe you do, but this guy knows whom you work for and what you do. You will create an impression on him that he will bring back to the nest. And his firm may very well wind up advising the officers of your organization.

On the other hand, do you go overboard in your desire to be friendly? For all you know, somebody in his firm is bidding on a contract with your company, and he is seeking information that will give his firm the advantage. You need to be careful about telling this person things that the organization doesn't want anyone on the outside to know.

Meanwhile, you have forgotten your wallet. The conductor comes around—it's the same conductor you've seen a thousand times—asking for your commuter ticket. You can humbly say, "I'm sorry. I forgot my wallet. I'll bring the ticket tomorrow, and we can double-punch it then."

Or you can be mean about your own mistake. "You know I'm good for it," you grouse. "You see me on this train every day. Now go punch somebody else's ticket."

The way you treat this guy who is just trying to do his job will do more to shape the impression you make on the lawyer next to you than anything else you do or say.

It's not even 8 o'clock yet, and you have already worried about how you dress, the way you ask a favor from the conductor, and how to maintain your reputation for discretion while appearing helpful and pleasant at the same time.

This "career warfare" stuff is exhausting. Before you even arrive at the office, you are already establishing your brand.

8:45 A.M.: MY KINGDOM FOR A CUP OF COFFEE

As you walk into your building, you say hello to the security guard and the receptionist—or you don't.

It's a small thing, but then again, small things can have a big influence on the impression you make on people in power. On my first day at John Hancock, my boss said to me, "I saw a lot of candidates for your job. And while you were chosen because you were the right fit, I'll tell you something. My secretary said to me that of all the people who came here, you were the nicest."

What if I had been rude to her? I probably wouldn't have gotten the job.

In most organizations, you cannot rise in power unless you can manage other people. To the higher-ups, what the receptionist thinks of you can seem like proof of your managerial abilities—or your arrogant lack of them.

> **Don't think that your behavior to players you consider peripheral does not matter. The way you treat a receptionist can be seen as proof of your managerial abilities.**

But on to more important questions. You have a staff meeting at 9 a.m. and you can't leave, but you still haven't had your first cup of coffee. How are you going to get one?

Obviously, you are going to ask your assistant to get it for you. Again, the way you ask will make an impression on him or her. Are you making this person feel little? Or do you offer a graceful exchange: "I'll get the coffee for us tomorrow."

9:00 A.M.: THE STAFF MEETING AND OTHER ANNOYANCES

You step into the conference room for the staff meeting that your boss holds every week. Frequently, these meetings are so breathtakingly boring that you spend the time hoping against hope that an oxygen mask will drop from the ceiling. You are in charge of something that you consider crucial to the organization—let's say, product development. Yet the big boss also oversees the cafeteria, so you inevitably have to sit through a scintillating report on the number of cookies that were baked that week.

It is a big mistake, however, to let boredom lull you into inattention. Meetings, after all, are the stage on which you build your brand—or demonstrate your worst qualities in front of an eager audience. Whenever I sit in a meeting, I feel like Ray Walston in *My Favorite Martian*. The antennae go way up.

> **Meetings are the stage on which you build or destroy your brand. Make sure your antennae are always up in them.**

Staff meetings can be particularly dangerous. In effect, you are meeting with the people who will be competing with you for raises and promotions in front of the person who decides how much money you make and whether your career goes up or down or out.

Regardless of how polite or how helpful your peers are, the environment is essentially predatory.

So what do you do when the boss turns to you and says, "How are things progressing in your department?"

Do you now hog the spotlight out of a desire to outshine everyone else? Do you decide that this is the moment to argue for something you really want from the boss, a new direction for your department?

Either one would be foolish. Both are contrary to the basic premises of a staff meeting.

There are three basic kinds of meetings whose dynamics you should comprehend: staff meetings, get-something-done meetings, and combat meetings—the meetings at which you are arguing for resources, money, or approval.

> **There are three basic kinds of meetings whose dynamics you should understand:**
> - **The staff meeting**
> - **The get-something-done meeting**
> - **The combat meeting**

Staff meetings are a classic show-and-tell with one purpose only: They are an efficient way for the boss to find out what is going on. Of course, he or she will use the excuse that everyone needs to know what is going on, but that is not the purpose of the meeting. For the most part, everyone but the boss already *knows* what is going on.

If you decide to use a staff meeting to argue for yourself or for a project, you are turning a meeting designed to serve the boss into something self-serving, and you will not be popular for it.

And if you go into too much detail about what you are doing or intend to do, you are giving the other people in

> **Do not use a staff meeting to argue for yourself or a project.**

the room an advantage over you that they don't need to have. After all, these people are competing with you for resources. If you offer them too much information too soon, you have only given them time to mount a campaign against your projects in favor of their own.

If you are smart, you say the minimum necessary to suggest that you are making progress without being specific, and you make yourself look like a team player by thanking everyone in the room who has given you any help.

Today, you are smart, and you get off the stage quickly. Unfortunately, as soon as you finish, your assistant finally appears with that cup of coffee you asked for.

Bad idea. You've instantly made yourself look like an elitist by asking someone to serve you in such a setting. And you've made every single person in the room mad.

You've annoyed the assistant because you've made him or her appear menial in front of powerful people. You've annoyed the boss because you have made him or her look cheap for failing to offer anything to the group. And everyone else in the room is annoyed because they want some coffee, too! The old Catholic school adage applies here: "Did you bring enough gum for everybody? If not, spit it out!"

At the very least, it would have been smarter to ask your assistant to leave the coffee outside, and then to discreetly slip out to get it.

Before you have taken three sips, you are asked to listen to your least favorite colleague. Let's call him Mr. Sigma Tau Gamma. He is a smug goody two-shoes—the same annoying frat guy you despised in college, just with a different name. Today, he has brought charts to support his dull ideas. You cannot believe that this guy is in the running for the same promotion you want.

Do you say something sarcastic? Do you pick a fight? Do you helpfully point out the flaws in the guy's plan, just like the kid in every school class who always has his or her hand raised even when someone else is talking: "Hoo, hoo, I have the answer?"

Bad idea. First of all, this is the wrong occasion to undercut a peer. Staff meetings are designed to make the boss feel good, the proud patriarch or matriarch of a great team. The last thing he or she wants to see is the kids fighting.

Second, if you build a reputation as someone who takes the gloves off at a moment's notice, you hardly seem circumspect or discreet—qualities you had better attach to your brand if you want the boss to trust you.

Third, if you embarrass someone in a meeting, you will make an enemy forever.

Fourth, you will create a reputation for treachery even among your better peers. Do not think this is not dangerous, even if you do not attack those peers directly.

I learned an interesting lesson once from a fish tank.

I had a roommate who kept freshwater fish and fed them about 15 goldfish a day. There were no two of the same species in the tank, but the fish could be divided into three groups. There were the high-swimming fish who got the food first, the frou-frou fish in the middle who took the remnants from the tearing of the flesh, and the bottom-feeders who waited until the other two groups had digested the goldfish.

Then one day, my roommate got bored with the fish and stopped feeding them. What happened was, the top swimmers moved on the frou-frou fish right away; and after they were gone, they moved on the bottom-feeders. Then things got interesting. There were six predators left, all different species. But soon it was five against one, then four against one, and so on. It was just a question of which one. Together, the remaining fish decided which predator they would weaken and kill, until finally only a single fish remained in the tank. And the roommate sautéed that one for himself.

That tank taught me that even unlike species will gang up to take out a dangerous competitor. And the same holds true in business. When Ann Godoff was fired as president of the Random House Trade Group in early 2003, the *New York Times* made her sound a lot like one of the pecked-at predators in my roommate's tank. According to the *Times*, she was ousted "at a time when her political underpinnings at the company were particularly weak because she had alienated some of her most powerful peers." Her counterparts at other Random House divisions reportedly felt that she looked down on them.

Beware of antagonizing your colleagues. They may very well decide that finishing you off is a matter of self-preservation for them.

Finally, attacking a peer is pointless. If you truly dislike the person and think he or she is worthless, chances are, nobody else likes or admires him or her either. And eventually he or she will self-destruct. On the other hand, if he or she really is smart and good at the job, attacking him or her will be held against you.

In the end, organizations are most comfortable with people who are not openly confrontational, but who demonstrate through achievement how much better they are.

Of course, as you have probably guessed from the tone of this book, learning to keep my opinion of my colleagues to myself was one of the harder

> **Do not develop a reputation for attacking your peers. If you think someone is worthless, chances are that he or she will eventually self-destruct. If he or she is really good at his or her job, on the other hand, an attack will only hurt your brand.**

lessons for me. When I was younger, I used to relish going after my counterparts at Control Data. I actually accomplished many times what they accomplished, but by denigrating them in public, I wound up hurting my own career a lot more than I hurt theirs. I created a label for myself that every ambitious person should try to avoid: too valuable to get rid of and too troublesome to promote.

When I demonstrated the same aggression toward my competitors at John Hancock, Steve Brown, my predecessor as CEO, gave me some excellent advice. He said, "Your competition can't hit an 80-mile-per-hour fastball, so why are you throwing 100? If you'd take 20 percent off your fastball, you'd be better off."

Of course, it takes a lot of self-discipline to refrain from pointing out the idiocy of an idiot. And today, you cannot resist saying something snide about Mr. Sigma Tau Gamma. It goes over like a lead balloon.

9:45 A.M.: REACH OUT AND TOUCH SOMEONE

Now it's a quarter to ten. You go back to your office, and there is already a pile of pink slips on your desk. You have to make a dozen phone calls, and you're in a rush.

You're irritated because you had to take the train this morning with that lawyer. You're irritated because you had to go to a stupid show-and-tell meeting that you could have done without. You're irritated at yourself for being rude to Mr. Sigma Tau Gamma. So far, the only good thing about the day is, you got coffee. But even that was a bad idea.

So you get on the phone and bark at everyone you talk to. Congratulations. By ten o'clock, you have made a terrible impression on another dozen people.

10:30 A.M.: YOU ARE GERTRUDE STEIN

It's time for another meeting with a different flavor and different rules. This isn't a show-and-tell like the staff meeting. It's a get-something-done meeting.

In this particular meeting, the group is trying to come up with some hot new products to introduce. The group includes engineers, marketing people, and salespeople, some of whom you know and some of whom you don't know. And, in contrast with the last meeting, you are now the highest-level manager present, the one who will be the audience for other people's presentations.

Whatever a get-something-done meeting is about—a new advertising campaign, a new software program, a new way of organizing the supply closet—it is essentially more relaxed than a staff meeting. The right-brainers or creative people dominate the play here.

> **In a get-something-done meeting, the right-brainers or creative people dominate the play.**

Your job is to be like Gertrude Stein, the American writer whose Paris home was a salon for artists like Hemingway and Picasso and whose "chance remarks," according to the *Encyclopædia Britannica*, "could make or destroy reputations." You have to be a bit of a despot to keep standards high, but not so much of a despot that you wind up crushing the free flow of ideas.

You are now chewing on a Styrofoam cup and listening to people prattle on about potential products. You don't like what you hear from two of the engineers. And you are tempted to show the strangers in the room how powerful and smart you are.

Do you ask the engineers why they are wasting your time? Do you tell them about your overpowering sense of *déjà vu*? Do you point out that every intellectually lazy engineer the organization has ever employed has proposed the same thing?

Again, you're creating an impression, especially with the people who don't know you and have no idea what you are capable of. They will walk away thinking either "This person's a leader" or "What a jerk." And if they think you are a jerk, that impression will get taken back to the nest, and everyone they work with will soon think you are a jerk, too.

You decide to do the better thing for your brand and compliment the engineers. "Look," you say, "I don't agree with all of this, but I think you guys have done a great job. I want to study it some more. I'm not sure that I'm going to do this, but I've learned over the years that taking some time helps."

Now, the people closest to you will know that this particular project is dead on arrival. Any time *anyone* in business says that he or she has to think about something, it is dead on arrival. That's the code. But you have left the presenters some dignity and have made a good impression on the rest of the room because of your courtesy.

However, it's not enough for your brand for you just to appear to be a polite person. You also need to generate some results. So you decide to let the conversation wander a little. This is smart. People need some freedom in order to come up with something new.

But before you let everybody off the leash, do you assert your leadership and set the goal? Do you say, "This is what we have to get done. Now let's be creative about how to do it"?

You'd better, because these meetings can go either way. I've been in many get-something-done meetings that have devolved into farce because the leaders failed to keep their eyes on what needed to be accomplished.

> **Get-something-done meetings can either devolve into farce or yield great ideas.**

For example, I was once employed by an organization that had gotten into real trouble and was desperate to cut expenses. Management had decided to run a contest asking the employees to come up with money-saving ideas. That was actually pretty smart, because who would know better how to save money than the people who were actually making the machine run?

So we needed to devise a reward system for the best money-saving ideas. The idea my group presented was very simple: We would give people a percentage of the money they had saved the company. Our program was basically a contract with the employees—a contract that any four-year-old could understand.

Our idea was well received, but by the time the final meeting on this subject had been held, another idea had been arrived at. The company would buy silver thistle pins. The chairman of the board, who was from America's "heartland," had some kind of affection for thistles. So, regardless of whether you saved the company a hundred dollars or a million, you would get this little trinket. Needless to say, management was not flooded with great ideas.

It happens all the time. In the intoxicating atmosphere of a get-something-done meeting, a serious endeavor deteriorates into a completely stupid result. And it invariably makes the person in charge seem foolish.

> To look like a leader when you're in charge of a get-something-done meeting, you have to be enough of a despot to keep people focused on a goal, but not so much of a despot that you crush the flow of ideas.

But you are on your game now. You manage to let people free-associate without losing sight of what has to be accomplished. The group comes up with some interesting ideas. You did a good job for your brand.

12:00 P.M.: THE LUNCH DISH

You're having lunch with a colleague from another division who used to work in your division. Does your good work at the product development meeting make you good company?

Or does your expansive mood encourage you to say too much? Do you end up doing what usually happens at these luncheons? Do you start bitching about the people you work with, or your bosses, or your projects?

Your colleague may seem like a sympathetic listener, since she once had to put up with the same nonsense. But how can you be sure that she won't take everything you say and find a way to use it in subsequent days?

> **To avoid a reputation for indiscretion or negativity, don't complain about your job to your colleagues.**

If she is not a trusted friend, she may well give you a reputation for being negative. In your business life, you will have thousands of luncheons with your colleagues. It is not smart to let your guard down there, either.

1:15 P.M.: THE BOSS THROWS A WRENCH

You rush back to your office and find a series of phone calls that have to be returned by 2:00. But the boss has left a message saying that he needs a report on his desk by 2:30.

Your whole schedule is blown. You call your subordinates for help.

Do you say, "The boss wants this done, so we need to push to get it done"?

Or do you bitch about the boss? This gives the people underneath you permission to bitch about your boss also, and they may not be discreet about where and when they do it. It also gives them permission to bitch about *you*. Every manager's behavior cascades downward, for better or for worse.

> **Every manager's behavior cascades downward, for better or for worse.**

You get the report done, and you continue with your day. Do you allow all

138

the inconveniences you've experienced to make you unpleasant, or do you just push through?

The professional person pushes through.

3:00 P.M.: THE COMBAT MEETING

It's gone from 6 a.m. to 3 p.m. in a blink. And now you have the kind of meeting that really represents a fight for your career—the approval or budget meeting that determines how much you are actually allowed to accomplish. If there is a dollar sign attached to a meeting, by definition, it is major league.

Today, you are trying to persuade a group of senior executives to spend $4 million to develop a prototype for a new product your group has come up with.

> **The real combat meetings are those that involve money or approval.**

Fortunately, you have every confidence that this is the right thing for the company to do. And you are a good enough presenter to convey that confidence to your audience.

But that does not mean that you shouldn't be prepared for every possible argument against it. I once made the mistake of assuming that just because something was logical, it would be approved. Years ago, I tried to persuade the powers-that-be to offer John Hancock customers non-Hancock brands of mutual funds through our insurance and annuity products. The market reality was that our customers were demanding more choice in their investments. However, I was unprepared for how violently our inside investment managers were going to react to the potential loss of assets for their own funds. And they wound up winning the day, though they eventually lost the war.

You need to be prepared for all meetings, especially combat meetings. It is not enough just to gather the information to make your case.

> **Be prepared for combat meetings. Make sure you understand the players and their agendas as well as the substance of your own argument.**

You should also do your best to know the people who will be in the room. Who's smart, who's not smart. Who's powerful, who's not powerful. Who has an agenda, who doesn't. And you need to be mentally ready for the possibility that someone will try to sabotage your plans.

Of course, the greatest danger in combat meetings is that you will sabotage yourself. This happens when you are either unwilling to admit victory or unwilling to admit defeat.

In the first case, you have basically won your point. I've been in a zillion meetings where the boss understood what someone was arguing

> **The most common way in which people sabotage themselves in combat meetings is by continuing to argue when it is time to either admit victory or admit defeat.**

for right away and said, "You know what, you're right. You don't need to tell me any more. I agree with you. You have $4 million to develop this project."

But instead of saying a gracious, "Thank you," some people will go on arguing, either because they haven't finished using all the points they have prepared, or because they decide to bludgeon everybody with their intelligence.

People who do this wind up boring their bosses and tempting them to change their minds.

Unfortunately, you don't have the opportunity to snatch defeat from the jaws of victory today. The boss says, "Not only do we not have $4 million for this project, but we think we are going to have to ask you to cut $4 million from your budget."

You have a choice. Do you go on arguing? Do you take a moral stand? If the decision has truly been made, you will only add some unpleasant attributes to your brand: recalcitrant and difficult.

Or do you accept the loss? Do you say, "I get the message. I'll come back in a week, and I'll tell you what I can't cut and what I can and what the consequences are"?

Today, something in your boss's tone tells you not to fight the inevitable, so that is exactly what you say. Smart. You now seem to be someone who is willing to sacrifice his or her personal ambitions for the greater good of the company. That is something that gets rewarded in organizational life.

> **Sometimes the best thing you can do for your brand is to accept bad news gracefully. You will be seen as someone who is willing to sacrifice personal ambitions for the good of the organization.**

3:45 P.M.: YOUR SUBORDINATES MESS UP

It's now 3:45, and some of your subordinates have come to see you because they are having a problem meeting a deadline you set for a research report.

Do you empathize and give them more time?

Or do you get mad and become unfair?

You get mad. You tell them you don't care how long it takes, you want it tonight. Now, you know you don't need it tonight. And they also know you don't need it tonight. Tomorrow night would be fine. But you decide they need to see a show of power.

Somebody says, "But I've got New York Knicks tickets for tonight!"

"Too bad," you say.

> **Your subordinates will know the difference between an urgent request and an empty show of power. The latter will hurt, not help, your brand.**

Fine. Just be aware before you say it that you will have made an enemy forever.

5:30 P.M.: ABSOLUT REWARD

You are finally out of the office and at a cocktail party for a local charity. You have already had one much-deserved martini, and the waiter offers you a second.

Should you take it? It's been a long day. Sure.

7:00 TO 11:00 P.M.: THE DYNAMO WINDS DOWN

You take an out-of-town client to dinner to talk about what she'd like to see your organization offer in the near future.

However, you can't quite grasp your thoughts because you have had a hair too much to drink. You are by no means drunk, and the client doesn't think you are drunk. She is just wondering what happened to the dynamic person she'd been told about.

Tomorrow, you are going to have to telephone her and try to correct this impression. But tonight, before you fall asleep, you decide to grade yourself on your performance. A mixed day, C plus at best.

During the day, you had 30 encounters and made an impression on 30 different people. It's possible that none of those encounters will mean anything in the long term for your brand. It is also possible that any one of them may tip the balance for your career. The maddening thing is that you rarely get any advance warning about which is which.

The truth is, no one handles every encounter perfectly. The best you can do is establish good patterns so that the occasional lapse from good judgment won't hurt you, and people will basically believe that you are the kind of person who can be trusted with a secret, an urgent project, or a promotion.

Since you are an ambitious person, right before you drift off, you promise yourself that you will do better tomorrow.

> No one handles every encounter perfectly. The best you can do is to establish good patterns.

7

MAKE THE
RIGHT ENEMIES

S o far, we have talked a lot about how foolish it is for someone who
is trying to build a successful brand to be gratuitously rude, mean,
or combative. And usually it is foolish.

But here is something that is equally foolish: trying to build a successful brand by never offending anyone. Even the attempt is guaranteed to turn you into mayonnaise, into beige wallpaper, into the kind of
white noise that only gets ignored in organizational life.

If you want the extra gestalt of an identifiable brand, you have to
decide at some point who you are and who you are not. And then you
have to take the hits that you will take for being yourself, because not
everybody is going to like you, that is for sure.

Sometimes you have to fight back against the people who do not
like you. Sometimes you even have to pick a fight with the people you

don't like. Sometimes you have to throw out all the rules and show yourself in a negative light for the sake of your own self-respect.

This chapter is not about when to be *gratuitously* rude, mean, or combative—it's about when to be deliberately so.

OUTRUN THE BASTARDS

Face facts. No matter how intelligent, hard-working, and well-meaning you are, you will make enemies in your work.

In fact, organizational life is a lot like every episode of every murder-mystery show that has ever appeared on television, from *Columbo* to *Law & Order*. The episode always starts with a body, usually that of a prominent and successful man or woman.

When the detectives show up, they always ask the widow or widower, "Did your spouse have any enemies?"

And the bereaved always answers tearfully, "No, he/she was a wonderful person. I can't think of anyone."

Of course, before the next commercial break, it becomes clear that the deceased had an *army* of enemies. And the rest of the hour is spent whittling a dozen suspects down to the one who actually did the deed.

In organizational life, you never really know how many enemies you have. But I guarantee, it is *always* a lot more than you and the spouse think you have. This may sound paranoid, but as Henry Kissinger famously pointed out, "Even a paranoid can have enemies."

You will make some enemies without lifting a finger, simply by virtue of who you are. You will make enemies because you are short or you are tall, or because you are a woman or you are a person of color. You will make enemies because of your education—either you didn't go to the type of school that's in favor now, or you went to a better school than your peers and will suffer because they are jealous. You will make enemies because you work for a certain department or for a certain individual who is the sworn enemy of someone else. You will make enemies just because you exist.

I learned this hard truth before I'd been in the working world more than a week. I was 21 years old, and I had just taken the second airplane ride of my life to Chicago for the 20th anniversary celebration of the public relations firm for which I now worked. It was awkward for me because I had just taken the job, and I didn't know anybody except the guy who had hired me.

At the party my first night in Chicago, I was glad to be introduced to a woman whose group I was joining. Let's call her "Elaine." She was in her late fifties, and she had been in the public relations business all her life. Like me, Elaine was an account executive, though, clearly, she made much more money than I did.

I said, "It's nice to meet you, Elaine."

The first words out of Elaine's mouth were, "I hope you don't expect any help from any of us."

"What do you mean?" I asked.

"Look," she said, "you're a kid, and I've worked 30 years in this business. But I'm at the same level they brought you in at. So don't ever come down to my office looking for any help."

I hadn't done so much as eat a sesame-encrusted cracker in front of her. But it didn't matter. Just my presence was enough to infuriate her.

The truth is, the first day you come into an organization, you will have more enemies than you have friends. Sure, the couple of people who hired you probably like you. But to everyone else, you are an outsider, and you may be threatening. So you're probably down 10 percent of the audience on the first day.

As you go on, you will make other enemies that you don't want to make, but that you have to make because some issue of substance is at stake. When I first arrived at John Hancock, for example, people in my department gave me the operative wisdom about the place. "Don't rock the boat," they said. "Try, try not to be noticed. Don't come up with any ideas that can be shot down. Don't call your boss. Only answer when he calls you. And you'll be able to get a good 25 years in."

Since this was not my plan—just treading water for 25 years—I soon made them very, very mad because I actually expected them to do more than just tread water, too.

In fact, you are especially likely to make enemies if you are ambitiously attempting to build a personal brand by taking risks, taking stands, making sure you are heard, and accomplishing big things. Some people will be jealous of you because the boss likes you; others will dislike you because they are afraid you will soon be the boss.

> **Face facts: You will make enemies in organizational life, and the more successful you are, the more enemies you will make.**

Success creates legions of sycophants, but it also creates legions of foes. And by the end of your career, you will be very lucky if your fan club is as large as the number of people who make up your base of enemies.

Ed Koch, the former New York City mayor, once said something to me about the detractors you gather along the way that I think is right: "You have to outrun the bastards."

What he meant was, if you stick around long enough, you are going to tick off various factions, and you may not be able to get them back on your side. You cannot gather even a modicum of power or influence without making some people angry.

> **If you make your bosses' lives better, your detractors usually won't matter.**

Of course, you'll have to try to limit the damage. You'll have to try not to make the union employees and the international management team mad in the same year. But the smartest strategy is to attain your next office before the people who have it in for you can drag you down. In general, if you concentrate on making your bosses' lives better, it will not matter if you leave a few disgruntled colleagues in your wake.

DON'T EXPECT GARY COOPER

There are times, however, when it is crucial for you to turn around and fight an assault on your brand, because your career will be finished if your enemies' point of view prevails. Unfortunately, you may not even be aware that your brand is in mortal danger.

In organizational life, it is almost never High Noon, where the guns are drawn in a public street. Instead, it's Scud missiles falling out of nowhere. It's the Borgia-style clinking of glasses, where poison gets spilled into your wine. It's a much more murky and complex game, with your assailants doing their best not to leave fingerprints.

In fact, in my entire career, I can think of only a single instance of a true High Noon–style confrontation. It was during the Olympic scandal of 1999, when some International Olympic Committee members were revealed to

> **Your enemies will rarely confront you directly. Instead, they will try to hurt you without leaving fingerprints.**

have accepted bribes in exchange for their votes for host cities. As an Olympic sponsor, I was very public with my dissatisfaction with the slow pace of reform at the IOC. NBC Sports chairman Dick Ebersol, who had paid billions for the right to broadcast the Olympic Games, thought my criticism was threatening his investment. So he arranged a conference call with reporters and told the world that I was a "two-bit bully" whose actions demanded this response: "Shut up."

At the time, I countered by calling his attack desperate and unprofessional. But I will give Ebersol some credit—he is one of the few people I've ever met who was willing to step into the street in that way. And in the intervening years, a degree of respect and friendship has developed between us, because of his willingness to simply say, "Draw."

I guarantee that very few of the enemies you meet in your career will have the courage to criticize you to your face, or on the record, as Ebersol did. Most of them will stay in the weeds where you cannot see them and try, instead, to destroy you with unsourced leaks to the press, gossip, and hints about your failings to those in power. Especially when they cannot get you on the merits, they will resort to rumor and innuendo to do you in.

> **When your enemies cannot get you on the merits, they will often try to destroy your brand with gossip.**

Losing political campaigns, for example, almost never wind down without a whispering campaign to the press, as the various players try to shore up their reputations as political strategists by savaging the reputations of the other players. I observed this personally as director of advertising for the 1988 Dukakis presidential campaign. Trying to shift the blame for what was turning into a debacle, one senior person kept running to Mike Wallace of *60 Minutes* to denigrate the rest of the campaign brain trust. The equivalent happened in the Dole presidential campaign of 1996; one political consultant said that if he were going to write a book about his experience there, he'd call it *The Snake Pit*.

Despite their surface politeness, businesses, too, can be snake pits, as I learned when I almost had a promotion derailed by gossip.

I had been named head of the division I worked for. But before I actually began my new job, the president of the company called me into his office and said, "Look, even though I've offered you this promotion, I think I've made a mistake."

I was shocked. "What's the problem?" I asked.

"The feedback," he said, "is terrible. People don't want to work for you."

I soon learned the source of his information. A guy whose boss I was about to become had been spreading unpleasant stories about me. He didn't want me as his boss. Life was good, and he was afraid I'd be more demanding than his current bosses.

So he said one of the worst things that could possibly be said about a manager: He said that I was unfair, someone who promoted people out of favoritism.

It happened not to be true, but that didn't matter. I was put in the terrible position of having to prove to the company president that I was indeed fair and that I promoted people based on performance. I literally had to show my statistics to him.

Fortunately, the statistics backed me up, so I did become this guy's boss. And I never, ever forgave him for trying to poison the well—or trusted him again.

Your coworkers will take shots at you for all kinds of biblical reasons: envy, greed, lust, sloth, you name it. The truly dangerous ones will do it simply for sport. And you may not always be as lucky as I was and have a boss who tells you outright what the rumors are doing to your brand. So it is smart to be attuned to the signs that someone is trying to do you in.

Those telltale signs include:

- It's taking longer for your phone calls to be returned.
- People you used to see easily are now frequently busy.
- Instead of greeting you with, "Hey, what's up?" people greet you with a super-sympathetic, "How are you doing these days?" It's a way of seeing whether you know yet that your days are numbered.
- Since people are not that imaginative and tend to repeat the bad things they've heard, suddenly they are all using the same metaphors about you.
- When you go to a cocktail party, the boss's spouse will barely look at you.

• Other people are extremely solicitous about your safety net, your health, and the health of your family. They want to assure themselves that you have something in the bank, that your spouse has recovered from his or her operation of a few months ago, and that you are in the pink—so that they can view your firing with a clear conscience.

> **Learn to recognize the signs that a campaign of gossip is being waged against you, and fight back.**

Do not allow your brand to be eaten away by your enemies' gossip. Find out what is being said, and fight it energetically.

NO MERCY FOR DISLOYALTY

It is important that you make the distinction between someone who openly disagrees with you and someone who tries to undermine your authority and bring down your career.

Criticism is not a betrayal. In fact, a willingness to disagree with you may be a sign of the most valuable form of loyalty—loyalty to the organization or the endeavor. It deserves respect, not retaliation.

An attempt to undermine your authority, on the other hand, deserves everything you can throw at it.

I already knew this at six years old, when I was in charge of our gang at recess. There were about 15 of us; and for some reason that I never understood, by first grade, I had gotten the assignment of deciding what we were going to do every day.

Some days, we'd play something called Toppies, where we'd throw baseball cards and see who would top whom at the end. Or we'd play a kind of baseball by hitting a rubber ball against the wall. Or we'd have a snowball fight, if the weather allowed. We'd be let out of the classroom onto the playground, and everyone would wait to see what I wanted to do.

One of the kids in my gang was a great little guy with a big nose and crossed eyes who eventually became a wonderful pianist. Let's call him "Tony." One winter day, Tony decided to revolt against my tyranny. He said, "I don't want to play with you any more. I'm going to play over here." And in the revolt, he cleaved off four kids into his own little gang.

I was very upset about these defections. But within a few days, Tony's gang wanted back into my gang. They said it wasn't any fun playing with Tony because there weren't enough kids.

Did I welcome them back? Absolutely not. They were out of the gang for the rest of the school year. I was six years old, but I froze them out without mercy. I already knew that banishment or death was the only reasonable punishment for traitors.

If you happen to be grown-up enough to have the power to *fire* the person who has betrayed you, you should.

A public execution done coolly and adeptly will not help you with the people who are already disloyal; it will not flush them out into the open. But it *will* help you with the people who were thinking about it. In a kindergarten class, there is always one kid who is really rebellious. Either the teacher gets that kid under control, or it's over. He or she has no authority with any of the other kids, either. It's the same in organizational life.

> **Make sure you fire traitors, as an example to everyone else.**

If the traitor is senior enough, you put out the right press release about his or her moving on to pursue other interests, and then let the act speak for itself. The one thing you have to remember is that the real reason someone is departing always makes it through the grapevine. People are very smart—they will make the connections. While legal constraints will almost certainly stop you from promoting the story, you should not go out of your way to dissuade others from the truth, either.

A reputation as an absolute pacifist is useful if you are a candidate for sainthood, but it's a disaster if you are a candidate for higher office in an organization. You have nothing to gain and a great deal to lose if you fail to make an example of someone who tries to undermine you.

SOMETIMES YOU HAVE TO THROW OUT THE RULES

Fortunately, your brand is not likely to suffer very much if you fight back against treachery, but it may well suffer if you are confrontational in other situations. Yet you may have to do battle anyway, just to maintain your self-respect. Sometimes you simply have to say, "All right, I'm going to endure a setback, but I have to live with myself."

We have talked about how foolish it is to alienate a boss, but there are times when you nonetheless have to do it. For example, I once had a boss who accused me of lying to him about something in my personal life. We had been quite close. We had traveled around the world together. But this was an ugly, terrible argument. That evening, I pulled out all the paperwork that proved that I had told him the truth. And in the morning, I took a fistful of papers into his office and threw them on his desk.

> **Sometimes you have to fight just to maintain your self-respect, even when you know it will hurt your brand.**

I said to him, "Don't ever ask me about my family again. Don't ever ask me how I feel. Do not speak to me again, ever, on any personal basis whatsoever."

And from that moment on, I never spoke to that man again except when work demanded it. We never shared a meal, never had a drink. I would never even travel on the same airplane as he did.

Eventually, he apologized and said, "I hope we can repair our relationship."

I was very clear about where I stood. "Not in this lifetime," I said.

He was my boss, but because he had questioned my integrity, I was willing to take the risk that freezing him out would hurt my brand. And it did set me back in some ways. My competitors could use it against me because they could talk to him and he wasn't talking to me. And everyone in the company knew that there was tremendous tension between us. It's like a husband and a wife who go out in public when they are not speaking. They think no one knows, but everyone knows instantly.

Ultimately, though, my problems with my boss made it clear, at least, that I was not a quitter. People said, "Whatever has gone on there, David is hanging in there professionally and doing his job." And it may have added as much to my brand as it took away.

> **Sometimes you even have to alienate a boss.**

Of course, what's far worse than treating a boss in a cutting manner is treating someone powerless that way. That is the definition of gracelessness, and it's sure to cost you the respect of everyone who learns about it. While you should always be good to the lower-level people in your organization, when you reach a certain elevation, you had better be extra good. But let me tell you about a time that I was not.

I was at a hockey game in a two-tiered company box. I was in the top box, another set of Hancock employees was in the box below, and there was a staircase joining the two boxes. So during one of the period intermissions, I went down the stairs and said hello to the people I knew. There were a couple of women I hadn't yet met, including a really, really big woman in a sleeveless muumuu. It was winter in Boston—in other words, cold—and we were sitting above an acre of ice, but she obviously had plenty of insulation.

"You're David D'Alessandro," she said to me. Then she added, with a note of menace, "I have a bone to pick with you."

People instantly gathered around us because they sensed that there was going to be a car wreck.

"You know," she said, backing me into a corner and starting to poke me, "this company used to be great until you joined it." Then she started in on what was really bothering her. "The prices in the cafeteria are becoming ridiculous. It's now 60 cents for a quarter-pounder with cheese," she said in a tone of towering outrage.

Six months before, I had been given a huge new set of responsibilities that included the cafeterias, which served 12,000 meals a day and were heavily subsidized. I was also a newly elected member of the company's policy committee and the board of directors, so I was trying to be extra careful in my deportment.

I civilly gave this woman the corporate answer. "We have been losing $3 million a year on the cafeterias. That's too much. What we are trying to do is keep our prices under the level you would have to pay if you left the building, without its costing the company so much."

She said, still poking me, "I don't care about that! Double french fries are now 50 cents!"

It was the poking that pushed me over the edge. "Well, apparently," I said, "the increased prices have not reduced your rate of consumption." And I managed to escape while she was trying to process that thought.

This story sounded much, much worse when it was retold with the finger in my clavicle omitted, and for the next four months I heard about it from *everybody*, from the mailroom people to the chairman. "Couldn't you have been more gracious?" was the consensus. "Did you have to pull out that kind of weapon with this poor woman?"

This is my point: I didn't *care* if my brand took a hit, because she was poking me and trying to embarrass me in front of other people. She had crossed the line and gotten what she deserved.

PROVOKE SOME GIANTS

The last kind of fight we're going to talk about sounds like the most suicidal of all: the unprovoked attack on someone who is truly powerful when you have nothing to gain personally and everything to lose. Clearly, this is not a smart thing to do just to be noticed. But there are times when even the most ambitious person really ought to throw rocks at giants, and that is when people weaker than you need a champion.

> **Don't be afraid to take on someone powerful if those weaker than you need a champion.**

Ted Turner, for example, probably did some good in 1996 and 1997 when he slung some unprovoked mud at the two richest men in the world, Bill Gates and Warren Buffett, for failing to give away enough of their fortunes. At the time, Gates was saying that it was not the right time of life for him to concentrate on philanthropy. Turner was having none of that: "They should do it no-o-ow!" he told Maureen Dowd of the *New York Times*.

By the end of 1999, Bill and Melinda Gates had donated $17 billion to their foundation and had announced major initiatives to vaccinate children in the third world and provide college scholarships for minorities here. I don't think the pressure from Turner hurt.

In my career, I've been provoked into taking on giants more than once. Here is one example: In March of 2002, I decided it was time for Cardinal Bernard F. Law of Boston to be held accountable for failing for years to protect children from the priests in his archdiocese who were known pedophiles. I wrote an op-ed demanding that he resign; this was before even the *Boston Globe* editorial board, whose own reporters broke the story about the way the church hierarchy handled pedophile priests, came out in favor of Law's resignation.

In response, there was a great surge from powerful Boston Catholics, who said, "You're right." There was also a great surge from powerful Boston Catholics who said, "How dare you?"

Soon after that, a friend of mine called and said he needed to see me as soon as possible. He sat in my office and began talking about things that were not urgent, which I found strange, but he was a friend. Then he said, "While I'm here. . ."

When someone says, "While I'm here," it really means, "*why* I'm here." My antennae immediately went up.

He said, "I was with the cardinal this morning. He's outraged about what you wrote. He said, 'How could he do this to me?'"

I just looked up from my desk. "You know, it's funny you should say that, because that is exactly the same question all those little boys asked of the cardinal's priests. And if you are indeed representing the cardinal, tell him I said that."

By the time the cardinal did resign in December of 2002, I was just one tiny voice among many. But speaking out ahead of the crowd was clearly a risk to my brand.

Some people will never forgive me for it. Nonetheless, doing it was a matter of self-respect. And, ultimately, self-respect has to be part of any good personal brand. Without it, you are too weak to be trusted.

If you have been paying attention up to now, it should be obvious that I believe that the best personal brands include courtesy, fairness, and tolerance. Building a reputation that is dominated by the adjective ruthless is dangerous: People start to wish that life would give you a dose of your own medicine.

> **Self-respect has to be part of any good personal brand.**

But a small dose of ruthlessness is healthy for a brand. You cannot be afraid to fight when you have to do so in order to protect yourself or the things you believe in. Let people know that you are benevolent when dealt with fairly but dangerous when roused, and they are certain to treat you with respect.

TRY NOT TO BE SWALLOWED BY THE BUBBLE

L et's assume that you have done everything right when it comes to your personal brand. You've developed the personal qualities that encourage people to trust you. The people you work with and for respect you. Increasingly, they turn to you for leadership. You are rising in the ranks. Life is good.

Congratulations. Now get ready to handle one of the greatest of all dangers for your personal brand: success.

If you don't think success is tricky, it is time to renew your subscription to *People* magazine. Flip through the pages of any issue, and you will be reminded that a surprising number of people self-destruct at the top: movie stars who take up shoplifting, famous authors who plagiarize, CEOs who oversee billion-dollar accounting frauds.

The most successful people sometimes do the most nonsensical things to destroy their brands. And "insanity runs in the family" is not the sole explanation.

Unfortunately, as delightful as attention, praise, money, and power are, they can also be isolating and unsettling. And they can be just as difficult to handle in your average ball bearing plant as they are in Hollywood.

In this chapter, we'll talk about the wrong way and the right way to deal with success on any scale, if you hope to be more than just another flash in the pan.

JUST ASK MARIE ANTOINETTE: IT'S DANGEROUS TO BE TREATED LIKE ROYALTY

When I first became an executive at one company where I worked, I was promoted into a new office, where I found three buzzers under the desk. I had no idea what they were for.

I pressed one, and a lady appeared.

"Who are you?" I asked. "What do you do?"

"I take correspondence," the lady said, "and deliver it to the person you want to receive it."

That was good to know, so I pressed another button.

A gentleman appeared. When I asked him what he did, he said, "I'm in charge of security on this floor. Let me know if you need anything."

Okay, I thought. What would the next good fairy do for me?

I pressed the third button, and another lady appeared. "I do personal errands," she said.

Apparently, I was not supposed to pick up my own dry cleaning any longer. I learned that day that being an executive is as close as any modern American will get to being royalty. You may not have 800 retainers and five castles, but you may very well have three people who appear at the push of a button to do your bidding.

Of course, not every workplace offers its executives buzzer-fairies— somehow we do without them at John Hancock—but it is almost inevitable

> **Becoming an executive is close to being royalty.**

that once you reach a certain level in any organization, you move in an atmosphere of entitlement.

If you want a cup of coffee, someone gets you one. If you want to reorganize your department or division, no one argues with you. For the most part, your every wish is law. And unlike politicians, who have to sing for their supper every few years, if you are even modestly successful in business, you can enjoy your power for a long, long time.

Thanks to the sycophantic tone of organizational life, you don't even necessarily have to rise particularly high to be treated with extreme deference. In the book *On a Clear Day You Can See General Motors*, automobile entrepreneur John DeLorean tells an outrageous story about a relatively low-level Chevrolet sales executive. The guy liked to have a refrigerator full of bedtime snacks when he traveled. When his underlings found out that a refrigerator wouldn't fit through the door of one hotel room, they took it upon themselves to put a crane on the roof and knock out the windows to get the refrigerator in. "It was," DeLorean notes dryly, "the most expensive midnight snack ever eaten by a GM executive."

You may not even have to pay your dues very long before you have your whims taken this seriously, particularly if you happen to be one of the spoiled children of the corporate world—a salesperson or an MBA. Salespeople, because they are generating revenue, tend to be treated with deference far out of proportion to their intellect or experience. And the MBAs tend to show up in the office right out of school and say, "Aren't you grateful that I'm here?" And out of exaggerated respect for their advanced training, people *are* grateful.

As much as you may enjoy the flattery and the perks, however, there are two problems with getting the royal treatment at the office.

First, it can be bad for your humanity. You get "yes-sirred" to death all day long. Then when you go home, if one of your kids says, "You know, Dad, I disagree with you," you tend to think he's being outrageously rude, because you have grown unused to being contradicted.

Second, it can be bad for your career. The more you are treated as someone exceptional by your organization, the more likely you are to believe that you *are* exceptional. The more you believe that you are exceptional, the more likely you are to believe that the rules don't apply to you—and the more likely you are to destroy your personal brand by breaking rules that *are* taken seriously by the rest of the universe.

Right there, you have the explanation for many a billion-dollar accounting fraud. In fact, if the implosions at Enron, Arthur Andersen, WorldCom, Tyco, and Adelphia demonstrated anything, it was that even pillars of the community succumb to the temptations of success.

Unless you are very careful, your achievements can nudge you into a kind of bubble that distorts your judgments. Since everything goes your way all day long, everything seems to confirm that checks and balances are for other people; you are free to do whatever you want.

> **There are two problems with getting the royal treatment at the office:**
> - **It can be bad for your humanity.**
> - **It can be bad for your career.**

That idea can make you very, very arrogant and very, very careless. You can wind up crippling your organization and shredding your reputation through some act you barely gave a thought to.

HOW TO HANDLE THE BUBBLE

The sad fact is, if you are successful in any field, it is impossible to avoid being drawn into the bubble.

No matter what you do, you will be subject to deferential treatment. You will have privileges other people won't. You will be flattered all day long. And these things will inevitably isolate you from the harsher realities of life and alter your eyesight in subtle ways. None of us really escapes.

Still, it is worthwhile to try not to be swallowed completely by the bubble. You can save yourself and your organization a great deal of trouble if you can force yourself to remember that, despite your exalted position, you are still subject to the rules of civilized society and the laws of the land. You are also accountable to your board of trustees or directors.

> You can't avoid the bubble completely. But it's worthwhile to try not to be swallowed by it.

Of course, most executives think that the way to keep their feet on the ground is by having coffee with 20 key employees once a month or visiting some distant offices to see what is happening in the field. The problem with that stuff is that it usually involves tremendous advance planning on the part of many people who are concerned with nothing but pleasing you. It's not real. It's staged to make it feel as if it's real.

Ceremonial events with the rank and file won't save you from your own ego.

Here are a few recommendations of things that might:

> **Six rules for avoiding the bubble:**
> 1. Be skeptical of your own genius.
> 2. Surround yourself with equally skeptical people.
> 3. Keep the friends who remind you that you're human.
> 4. Have some sympathy for your victims.
> 5. Develop interests other than golf.
> 6. Remember who feeds your family.

1. BE SKEPTICAL OF YOUR OWN GENIUS

If you have power, you are going to have your share of yes-people around you. Their praise can make you both arrogant and foolish. Skepticism helps. I always think, "I've never met anybody who could be right that many times in a row. So there must be something wrong here."

In baseball, you can fail seven out of ten times at the plate and still make it to the Hall of Fame. In business, most CEOs think they bat .900. Personally, I'm happy to bat .500. And I never believe anyone who tells me I'm right all the time.

2. SURROUND YOURSELF WITH EQUALLY SKEPTICAL PEOPLE

As much as you have the power to do it, create an environment of accountability in your department or division or company that applies to everyone—even you, the boss.

Instead of hiring only sycophants who think that the rules don't apply to you, hire some skeptical types who would enjoy nothing better than double-checking everything you do. If you're smart, you will have other people scrutinize your expense accounts before you sign them. And any top executive who doesn't have a good relationship with a lawyer whom he or she consults on a regular basis is a fool.

If you become CEO, there are actually people whose job it is to serve as checks and balances to you—your board of directors, your outside accountants, and your CFO. Don Keough, the retired COO of Coca-Cola, reminisced to *Fortune* that before the Enron–WorldCom era, CFOs used to be "tough, smart, and mean. . . . Bringing good news was not their function. They were truth-tellers."

Demand that your gatekeepers be truth-tellers, too, and that they push back whenever they see a lapse in judgment on your part. Make sure you welcome a board of directors, the majority of whom are independent—individuals who are from a sufficiently different line of work that they can offer you some perspective on your own little corner of the world.

Invite your board members to question you. Encourage them to meet without you present. Ask their advice as individuals. Not only will independent-minded directors help keep *you* out of the bubble, they will help keep your entire organization out of the bubble.

3. KEEP THE FRIENDS WHO REMIND YOU THAT YOU'RE HUMAN

If you are successful, it is easy to move into a world of Stepford executives and their spouses, where nothing bad ever happens and the grass is always as manicured as it is on a golf green.

Spend too long in executive-land, however, and you will probably forget all about ordinary life. That can help you mismanage your personal brand into infamy.

The problem with hanging out only with other executives is that all the talk is Big People talk: "Gee, the market's terrible." "What are we going to do about Congress?" Not one of these executives is going to say to you, "My mom is sick." They are not going to talk to you about anything emotional. That would be seen as a sign of weakness. And they will judge you on your earnings and your ability to recognize the pickle fork, rather than on what kind of parent you are.

It's important to remember that while you may be omnipotent in the office, you are just as subject to the eternal problems of human life as anyone else. Keep people around you who will talk to you about human things and remind you of this fact, and you may survive success with your judgment largely intact.

4. HAVE SOME SYMPATHY FOR YOUR VICTIMS

All executives have to do unpleasant things. Sometimes we have to limit spending. Sometimes we have to deny people raises. Sometimes we have to fire people.

Sometimes we have no choice about these things, but it is nonetheless important that we do not forget how to feel. One of the problems with the top jobs in business is that they are numbing. The people you answer to—analysts and investors—are "quants." They want the numbers. And striking a balance between some form of humanity and making the numbers is often hard.

But it can be done. You can be a tough executive without turning into Marie Antoinette. Try to remember that "Let them eat cake" is not an acceptable sentiment when you hold people's livelihoods in your hands, and you will make better decisions in the end.

5. DEVELOP INTERESTS OTHER THAN GOLF IN YOUR LEISURE TIME

Let me tell you about some of my unusual pastimes. I grow tomatoes and pumpkins and make candles. I work with my hands. On Sunday afternoons, I don't watch the Masters, I watch the History Channel.

Those are the things I do when I'm away from the office, not a recommendation for anyone else. Here is what I do recommend: Do something with your leisure time that reminds you that the world is bigger than your corporate kingdom. It will keep you from becoming a fool.

6. REMEMBER WHO FEEDS YOUR FAMILY

You can learn a lot by spending your childhood sleeping in a closet right above the family grocery store. When I was little, the fruit and vegetable supplier would come once a week and bring in a crate of oranges.

We didn't sell them by the pound; we sold them by the piece. My grandfather would always ask how much they were and then instantly do the math in his head to figure out the price he needed to charge for each orange in order to make a profit.

Once day, the guy told him a higher price than usual.

My grandfather said, "Put them back on the truck."

The man was very surprised. "You always get a crate of oranges every week!" he said. This was an Italian community, and fruit is very big with Italians, so the supplier didn't understand.

My grandfather said, "What good are they, if my customers won't pay for them?"

That was an interesting lesson for me. My grandfather knew his customers so well that he knew exactly how much they would be willing to pay for an orange—and at what price they would leave the oranges to mold in the crate. He also knew exactly whom he needed to please. It was not himself, and it was not the fruit supplier; it was the people who put the money in the till.

Unfortunately, this is an easy lesson to forget. We've built a society where if you are reasonably successful, you can wall yourself off from virtually anything—especially from those people who pay the bills.

I had almost forgotten about my grandfather and the oranges until I took a vacation in Maine in late 1988 to try to recover from the mental wounds I had sustained while working for the Dukakis presidential campaign.

I was in a Sears store in Brunswick, Maine, and there were two blue-haired ladies at the counter in front of me. One of them was talking about whether she could afford a little tiny pair of shoes for her granddaughter and asking the other's advice.

I realized with a shock how long it had been since I'd been around anybody with an IQ of under 140 or anybody who was not preoccupied with incredibly vast issues such as the death penalty, the country's economic well-being, how to avoid another hostage crisis, or what to do about unemployment.

I also promised myself that as a matter of self-preservation, I would never again forget about those ladies who were weighing price versus benefit in a pair of baby shoes.

The truth is, if you lose touch with the people who actually buy whatever it is your organization sells or who hold stock in your company, you lose sight of what is important. You lose your instincts for products and marketing. You forget to ask the right questions. You lack any sense of where your organization should be going. Inevitably, you screw up both your company's brand and your own.

> **Don't lose touch with the people who feed your family: your customers and your shareholders.**

People say that it's important never to forget where you come from. That's debatable. What's *really* important is to remember who is feeding your family. It certainly is not you alone, through the magnificence of your genius.

It's your customers and shareholders.

So never forget that while you may be the top banana in your office tower, you are still accountable to quite a crowd outside—to the many people who own your products and to the many people who own your stock. They give you your livelihood, and you'd better give them your loyalty and attention in return.

BUILD GOODWILL OUTSIDE OF YOUR OWN TINY KINGDOM

The people who build truly great brands are not those people who think that success exempts them from the rules that the rest of the world lives by. Instead, they are the people who use their success to connect with the rest of the world.

It is smart to go out of your way to win the approval of the community around you. This is important, not just for your own brand, but also for the brand of the organization you work for. If you are well liked, people are inclined to think better of the company you represent—and to give it the benefit of the doubt. That, right there, can mean the difference between success and failure for any endeavor.

> **Three powerful ways to build goodwill:**
> 1. Treat the press respectfully.
> 2. Work very hard to make your organization successful.
> 3. Give back.

Let's talk about how to build that goodwill.

1. TREAT THE PRESS RESPECTFULLY

When you reach a certain stage in your career, the press is going to want to talk to you about what you are doing. Initially, you may start fielding calls from stringers at industry trade publications or the local free paper. Eventually, if you are very fortunate or very unfortunate, it may be Bob Woodward on the line.

As a general rule, you and your organization should cooperate with reporters. After all, these are the people who paint your brand and your organization's brand for the world at large. Convince them that you are generous with your time and insights and unafraid of answering their questions, and the portrait is likely to be positive.

Of course, there is always a risk in talking to reporters. Eventually, if you receive enough favorable press, there will also be some negative stories. Over time, 80 percent positive stories to 20 percent negative is a healthy ratio. Of course, there is no politician on earth who would refuse an 80-20 split at the polls. Unfortunately, too many politicians, executives, and celebrities consider a split like that unacceptable when it appears in the newspapers. They forget that there is something called the First Amendment that allows the press to criticize them. And so, burned once, they treat the press with contempt or try to shut the press out.

In general, treating the press badly is a slow form of brand suicide. The great negative example of all time—a lesson in how not to do it— is Richard Nixon. Thin-skinned and resentful by temperament, Nixon decided very early in his political career that the press was his enemy and treated it accordingly. In 1962, after he lost his race for governor of California, Nixon gave a concession speech that was remarkable in its bitterness. "You've had a lot of fun—a lot of fun," he told the assembled reporters. "You won't have Nixon to kick around any more."

He would, of course, be wrong about that.

Even as a presidential candidate and then as president, Nixon allowed the national press as little access to him as he could possibly get away with, as Joseph C. Spear points out in his book *Presidents and the Press: The Nixon Legacy*. Nixon was not just evasive, he was sometimes openly insulting to the press, and, in secret, he kept a list of reporters who had given him trouble. When the Nixon administration's credibility was finally destroyed by Watergate, the press responded with years of pent-up rage and frustration—to the point that, according to Spear, reporters "hooted and jeered" during the daily White House press briefings.

Even in his grave, Nixon's terrible relationship with the press is still hurting him. In part, it explains why he is remembered more for his transgressions than for his accomplishments. The press is *still* kicking Nixon around.

If you resent having journalists prying into your business, my advice is, get over it. The truth is, while you may occasionally be faced with an unscrupulous journalist, in general, most journalists are ethical. If they are asking you questions you don't like, it is generally because they have a job to do.

This does not mean that you have to respond positively to every single request for an interview or answer every question or give out confidential information. Journalists, too, sometimes forget that we have a First Amendment. "Freedom of speech" means that you, too, get to choose when to talk and what to say.

It also does not mean that you have to talk to the few reporters who turn out to really have an ax to grind or to be incompetent. Or that you should try unduly to collect column-inches on yourself. I am not a subscriber to the theory that as long as they spell your name right, any publicity is good publicity.

It just means that you are generally better off if you work with reporters rather than against them. They are a group to be contended with, not a group to be feared.

If you resent journalists prying into your business, get over it. You are much better off working with reporters rather than against them.

When to say no to journalists:
- **When you don't have time to answer every interview request**
- **When they want you to reveal confidential information**
- **When the reporter is the rare exception who really has an ax to grind**
- **When the reporter is the rare exception who really is incompetent or unethical**
- **When you are just trying to satisfy your own vanity by collecting column-inches**

Stick to the facts when you talk to reporters. Don't get emotional. Remember that you are not on trial. Remember also that you cannot control the story. You may have astounding good news that is played small because the publication does not have as many advertisers that month and cannot afford to run as many pages. You may have minor bad news that is played large because it is summertime and not much else is happening.

Just understand that if you have achieved a certain prominence, the scrutiny comes with the territory.

Finally, demonstrate some courage. Step out and talk with reporters even when your organization is announcing bad news. Don't conceal yourself behind the skirts of your public relations people. If you have to fire people, make sure the quote as to why you are doing it comes from you.

Ultimately, you have a choice: Do you want your public image to be based on rumor and innuendo? Or do you want it to be based on access to you, so that you have at least a chance to influence the outcome?

In most cases, access is the safer way to go.

Despite their notorious bloodlust for the next great story, journalists actually are human. If you have established yourself over time as someone who is reliably helpful to them, they are likely to treat you with respect and gratitude. Ideally, they will even convey that respect to their readers, listeners, and viewers.

---

2. WORK VERY HARD TO MAKE YOUR ORGANIZATION SUCCESSFUL

It's very simple: Build something the world admires, and you will build goodwill. George Steinbrenner is someone who rehabilitated a very problematic brand largely by figuring out how to win.

In his first 20 years as principal owner of the New York Yankees, Steinbrenner was the perfect example of an executive who behaved as if the rules did not apply to him. In 1974, he pleaded guilty to making illegal corporate contributions to the Nixon reelection campaign. In 1990, he was banned from day-to-day Yankees operations for paying a gambler $40,000 to uncover embarrassing facts about outfielder Dave Winfield. His shortcomings as a boss were infamous. He changed managers at the drop of a hat and feuded with his players.

He clearly made plenty of mistakes out of arrogance. But during the 1990s, he altered his management style, becoming more patient, paying more attention to the farm system, and interfering with his managers less. As a result, the Yankees were able to win four World Series between 1996 and 2000.

As *New York Times* sportswriter Buster Olney put it, "All this winning has been good for Steinbrenner's reputation." Grateful New Yorkers stopped seeing Steinbrenner as an impossible tyrant and started seeing him as a lovable curmudgeon—not flawless, certainly, but someone whose heart was in the right place.

If you build something that people can readily respect, your shortcomings, too, will come to be seen as the exception to the rule, not the rule itself.

If you are part of a losing effort, on the other hand, no one is going to make any allowances for you. This was another lesson I learned from Michael Dukakis's 1988 presidential campaign. I joined the campaign six weeks before the election to try to salvage an inept advertising effort. After the election, I took a public pummeling. The press said the advertising was terrible—which it was. However, no one wanted to hear why. We were losers, and I just had to put up with my round in the barrel.

> **If you build something that people can respect, they will make allowances for your shortcomings.**

Of course, Brand Steinbrenner has a few other things besides success going for it. One is that the Boss has long been a soft touch.

3. GIVE BACK

Steinbrenner has done many charitable things over the years, particularly for children. He has been charitable on a small scale as well as a large. He reportedly once came across a deaf boy who was trying to get the players' autographs. Steinbrenner sent him to Memorial Sloan-Kettering to try to restore his hearing.

Steinbrenner has said simply, "I live OK because I work hard, but when I see a need is there, I like to give."

Liking to give is always a sympathetic trait. But cultivating that trait is crucial as you become more prominent and successful.

If you don't give something significant to your community, whether it's your money, your time, or your influence in supporting good causes, and if you don't do all you can to make sure that your organization gives something significant to the community as well, you will appear ungrateful. People will root for you to fall.

Finding yourself in trouble after *not* having done good for your community and *not* having supported good causes is one of the worst positions you can possibly be in. Former Sunbeam CEO Al Dunlap—also known as "Chainsaw Al" for his ruthless style as a corporate turnaround specialist—is the perfect example of someone who ran into trouble with very little goodwill in the bank. Dunlap seemed to be proud of his own willingness to fire thousands of people, and he openly scorned the idea that

> **The more successful you are, the more important it is for your brand to give of your time, money, and influence.**

corporations should give to the community, eliminating corporate philanthropy at both Scott Paper and Sunbeam. When he was fired as CEO by Sunbeam in 1998, there was practically a parade in celebration. John Byrne of *BusinessWeek* reported, "Rarely does anyone express joy at another's misfortune, but Dunlap's ouster elicited unrestrained glee from many quarters."

On the other hand, good citizenship that seems to be blatantly defensive will not help your brand, either. Mid-scandal is definitely not the moment to be talking about your charitable activities. By then, either you have a positive history or you don't. If you do, your good deeds will speak for themselves. If you don't, the world is suspicious of deathbed converts who turn into philanthropists on the advice of their public relations people.

So give for the right reason. Give because the world has made you prosperous and successful, and you owe it a debt.

Ultimately, philanthropy can help rehabilitate a damaged personal brand—but only if you demonstrate a steadfast commitment to a good cause long after the bad press has faded. Bill Gates offers the best possible example of this. Gates has helped a lot of people forget about the Microsoft antitrust case with his quiet moving of

> **How to give well:**
> - **Give because it's the right thing to do**
> - **Give where you can make a difference**
> - **Give locally**
> - **Give personally**

mountains to get people in the third world immunized. In 2003, the Global Alliance for Vaccines and Immunization told the *New York Times* that Gates had enabled it to save more than 100,000 lives in just three years.

A few other rules for building goodwill by supporting good causes:

- Give where you can make a difference. If you have the resources of Bill Gates, you can improve the health of entire continents. If your resources are smaller, try to have as profound an impact as Gates in a smaller arena.

- Give locally. The place to which you owe the greatest debt of gratitude—and the place where you most need to cultivate goodwill—is your own backyard.
- Give personally, using your own time and money also.

BUILD A RESERVOIR THAT YOU CAN TAP IN TIMES OF DROUGHT

Be generous with your time, money, power, insight, and efforts because you are a success now and *should* be generous. But also be aware that one of the side effects of this generosity is that both you and your organization will have some insulation from the mistakes you will make down the road.

Citigroup chairman Sandy Weill is a prime example of an executive who was smart enough to build a reservoir of goodwill long before he seemed to need it. By the time Citigroup was implicated in the excesses of the high-tech stock boom and forced in 2003 to contribute $400 million to a regulatory settlement for conflicts of interest on Wall Street, Weill had done many things right for many years. He had talked regularly to reporters. He had built what is often called "the most profitable corporation in the world." He had been one of the country's great philanthropists.

Weill was nonetheless voraciously attacked in the business press. And his personal brand took enough of a hit that he was forced to withdraw from consideration for a spot on the board of the New York Stock Exchange.

But here is what did not happen to Weill: Unlike a lot of the other players in the corporate scandals of that moment, he did not win a spate of editorials calling him Simon Legree.

In July of 2003, Weill announced that he would be passing the CEO's baton to Charles Prince. The story could have been played as if

Weill were a damaged executive escaping the weight of alleged organizational misconduct. Indeed, a few newspapers did spin it that way. Generally, however, Weill was treated warmly, as a towering figure in American business, and the alleged misconduct was just one of many subheads. The *New York Times* even devoted an editorial to Weill that made sure that no one would forget "his spectacular philanthropy."

> **Build goodwill in good times, because you will need that goodwill in bad times.**

Take a cue from Weill, one of the smartest businesspeople in history. Start building an excess of goodwill today, and your mistakes, too, may wind up as mere subheads in a great career.

"What mistakes?" you may say. Well, every prominent person and every organization makes them eventually. In the next chapter, we'll talk about handling public criticism intelligently, once you do provoke it.

THE HIGHER YOU FLY, THE MORE YOU WILL BE SHOT AT

L et's assume that you have avoided the worst excesses of arrogance, the real brand destroyers. Unfortunately, you cannot expect that just because you do not behave like an outlaw, your brand will never be publicly criticized. It doesn't take a crime or some extremely immoral act to generate negative news. Under the right circumstances, all it takes is the fact that you spend too much money on your hairdresser, or you launched a product that nobody likes, or you regularly play racquetball on company time.

Everybody makes mistakes, and everybody does well-intentioned things that look like mistakes. And the more your profile has been heightened by success, the more likely it is that any mistake or even perceived mistake you do make will get a broad airing.

It's very simple: The higher you fly, the more interesting it is to shoot at you. Your embarrassments, both personal and professional, become news. Do people care if a White House intern is having an affair with another White House intern? Outside of the involved parties, no. But if the President of the United States is having an affair with a White House intern, well, now, that is interesting. And it's even more interesting if he lies about it.

Bill Clinton is, of course, an extreme case of someone who seemed to enjoy flying high without a parachute. However, I don't know of a prominent person in any field whose brand has not been a target at some point or other. This includes university presidents, the heads of nonprofit organizations, movie stars, professional athletes, and arts impresarios as well as politicians and business leaders. It simply comes with the territory.

> **Once you reach a certain level of prominence in any field, bad press comes with the territory.**

If you are successful, you will generate widespread criticism at some point. You will be slammed in the newspapers. You may be sued. And it will not be fun. It will feel like having a woodpecker sitting on your head. No matter what you would rather be thinking about, there is that painful pounding to distract you.

However, you can take heart from the long list of prominent people who have been publicly thrashed at some point in their careers but nonetheless remain at the top of their game—people like CBS anchor Dan Rather, Hollywood leading man Hugh Grant, United States Senator Hillary Rodham Clinton, Microsoft chairman Bill Gates, radio crank Don Imus, and many others.

If you are an ambitious person, my advice to you is to prepare for bad news right now. Sooner or later, you will face unpleasant headlines. If you are lucky, the story will only make the rounds verbally within your organization. If you are less lucky, you will appear on the front page of the *New York Post* wearing a five o'clock shadow and a new nickname that no one will ever forget. If you handle the attack well, you can turn what might be a year-long story into one that lasts a few weeks and inflicts no lasting injury on your brand. If you handle the attack brilliantly, you may even come out of your trial by fire with your brand enhanced.

In this chapter, we are going to talk about avoiding and handling bad press. However, even if you have not yet reached a level where the press is very interested in your doings, many of the same principles apply to scrutiny coming from within the organization.

Here are the rules for minimizing the damage from any negative story and maximizing your chances of turning adversity to your advantage.

UNDERSTAND WHEN, AS RICKY SAID TO LUCY, "YOU GOT SOME SPLAININ' TO DO"

The best way to handle a negative news story, by far, is *not* to have to handle one in the first place. You can save yourself and your organization a great deal of trouble by explaining things to the world before they become problems. If your critics feel that they have discovered some information that you would rather hide, that is very different from their hearing the same information from you. Forthrightness is disarming.

Of course, it's easy to say "anticipate trouble" and hard to actually do it. Let me tell you my painful experience.

In the spring of 2003, John Hancock reported in its annual proxy statement that my pay package was $21.7 million. Suddenly, we were con-

> **Preventing negative news is the best course. Explain things to the world before they become problems.**

fronted with headlines crying, "Hancock Chief Takes Home $21.7 Million in a Bad Year." I got beaten up in both the local and the national press. While some people understandably believe that no one deserves that kind of money, I was beaten up in large part because of a misunderstanding of the various components of the package and the rationale behind them.

Although our compensation disclosures satisfied the company's legal obligations, we should have been more sensitive to the need to provide a fuller explanation of this very complicated subject up front. That way, we could have avoided responding to questions in the midst of a fast-moving story that, once in circulation, seemed to grow its own tentacles. As it was, despite our earnest efforts, we weren't able to satisfactorily head off certain misinterpretations of the facts.

The first fact: $21.7 million for 2002 was not an accurate synopsis of my pay package. Hancock doesn't look at compensation on an annual basis, but seeks to reward and promote the building of long-term value. Accordingly, the vast majority of the $21.7 million, reflecting the company's very strong performance in multiple years, was made up of either long-term incentive payments or restricted stock.

The second fact: The SEC requires that the full value of unvested restricted stock be posted up front in the proxy statement's summary compensation table at the time of the grant—unlike many other long-term incentives, which are only reported in the table years later, when cash gets paid out. So a lot of people were confused by an apples-to-oranges comparison.

The third fact: By anybody's standard, our board's compensation committee is a model. It is entirely independent, it meets up to ten times a year, it meets without management present, and it hires whatever outside experts it likes, including a compensation consultant, to advise it. Further, the compensation committee chose a particularly forthright form of compensation for Hancock top executives, one that had to be prominently disclosed to investors long before it was paid out (if indeed it was ever paid out).

There were lots of things that we could have said and should have said. After all, $21 million was a lot of money, and it was understandable that some people wanted more of an explanation. We just blew it. We never should have let a fuller, more nuanced story get buried in uninformed outrage.

THE BUNKER WON'T WORK FOR YOU ANY BETTER THAN IT WORKED FOR EVA BRAUN

Now, let me tell you what we did right: We never tried to lie about the issue, cover it up, or minimize it. We did not try to shake the story off as unimportant. No one said, "I want to focus on my salad"—Martha Stewart's now-infamous brush-off after she was asked about her ImClone stock sale on the CBS *Early Show*. We invited a leading Wall Street analyst to Boston so that we could answer her questions. We put the chairman of our compensation committee out front and center to explain the committee's intentions—which he did very eloquently.

We might have missed an opportunity to explain things more thoroughly in advance, but we patiently laid everything out afterwards. Once you generate a negative story, you will be living with it for a long time, so you might as well take the time to convey your point of view on it.

Of course, once a story has broken, even if you do explain yourself, you probably will not immediately recover the ground that your personal brand has lost.

Never underestimate the force of a simple argument against you: Did you or did you not get paid this amount of money? What did the president know and when did he know it? When did you stop beating your wife? These "common-denominator" arguments—which usually involve lust, greed, power-madness, or some combination of the three—are so compelling that people do not want to be dissuaded from them.

For example, once it's revealed that you had your company buy you a $6000 shower curtain—as Dennis Kozlowski, the Tyco CEO who was prosecuted for allegedly looting the company, apparently did—what could you possibly say that would alter the impression that makes? Even if your decorator explains that it was actually a $6000 upholstered *partition*, as Kozlowski's decorator did, what then? Would that convince a single person that you were not carrying on like Caligula? Probably not.

In my case, all the painstaking explanations in the world were not going to win over the guy who shoved me as I was walking across Dartmouth Street in Boston and snarled, "Somebody making that much money should have a car and driver."

> **Once a simple argument against you has been launched in the press, you cannot expect to defeat it with complicated explanations. But you have to explain anyway.**

Nonetheless, one of the worst things you can do is go into a bunker and not explain. The original story against you is like a river. It is going to run its course, and there is not much you can do to block the channel. The really significant question is, can you stop the tributaries from pouring in?

If you are not careful, as soon as the original story breaks, the press will be on to a dozen other potentially embarrassing stories about you, and everyone in town who never liked your face will be contributing to the torrent. Piling on has become the modus operandi. And the "aha!" factor brings out a lot of peculiar stuff.

In the midst of our compensation story, one reporter called me and said, "I understand that your office has a secret passageway up to a place where you have a large private gym with a sauna and a hot tub." Strange, but untrue. However, he was ready to run with the story.

What's unnerving about these attacks is the relative speed with which they pick up steam. They may start with the professional and move on to the personal, or they may start with the personal and move on to the professional—and sometimes nothing is left standing at the end.

How do you stop the secondary streams from flooding the river and washing your brand out permanently? At least some of them will never get started if you have built enough goodwill into your brand over the years.

And some will dry up instantly if you are perceived as being sufficiently forthright and reasonable in response to the questions you are asked—and if you find a way to correct your problems quickly.

> **Behaving in a forthright manner after a bad story breaks usually will not completely undo the damage to your brand. But it will probably keep the story from spreading.**

Of course, while it is crucial that you be open and honest, that does not mean that you have to go over the same facts dozens of times. Explaining yourself decisively once or twice should be sufficient.

It also does not mean that you have to answer every question a journalist or Wall Street analyst asks you. It may actually be illegal to say certain things. Other disclosures may hurt your family, your friends, or your organization unnecessarily. Xerox CEO Anne Mulcahy, for example, won high marks for turning Xerox around and for honestly acknowledging the company's problems. However, she herself expressed regrets for telling analysts in 2000 that Xerox had an "unsustainable business model." The stock dropped 26 percent in a single day in response.

When you are fighting a negative news story, a certain amount of discretion is necessary and will be respected. But if you seem to be concealing the relevant facts just to save your own hide, your brand is finished.

If you retreat to the bunker and refuse to explain yourself, the story changes subtly and poisonously. It is no longer about a particular mistake that you made, it is about your unwillingness to address the mistake. That leads people to suspect that your personal history is riddled with similar mistakes. And suddenly every unfortunate thing you ever did in your life is news.

Former U.S. Representative Gary Condit is a prime example of someone whose retreat to the bunker destroyed his brand. Once so popular that his California congressional district was referred to as "Condit Country," he lost his popularity after a 24-year-old Washington intern named Chandra Levy disappeared. Levy's distraught family said that Condit was not telling the full truth about what Condit eventually admitted was a "close" relationship with their daughter. The Washington police suggested that he was not completely forthcoming with them, either. "It took us three interviews and a lot of effort to get as far as we got," Washington's deputy police chief told the Associated Press.

The perception was that Condit had hindered efforts to find the young woman in order to protect his own image. Suddenly, the flight attendant who had allegedly had an affair with him was telling journalists her story, everything from Condit's hairstyle to the question of whether he was a murderer was openly debated, and his political career was finished.

> If you seem to be concealing information just to save your own hide, your brand is finished.

If Condit had opted to forgo the bunker, his brand might have survived.

PUBLIC PERJURY IS A BAD IDEA

Of course, even worse than a refusal to explain yourself is an out-and-out lie. A public lie can unleash an infinite number of tributaries. It no longer matters how outrageous or improbable the story may be. It is likely to be taken at face value. You cannot refute anything, because you have no credibility.

Only Bill Clinton and Monica Lewinsky, for example, know for certain whether the infamous cigar story she told the Independent Counsel's Office was true. But at that point, she could have said anything about their affair, even "Bill Clinton made me put on a Tweety Bird costume." His credibility was shredded to the point where anything was believable.

There have not been many political sex scandals as embarrassing as Clinton's—but that of U.S. Representative Barney Frank came close. However, it played out very differently because Frank handled it differently. In 1989, a prostitute named Steve Gobie who had had a sexual relationship with Frank claimed that he had run an escort service out of Frank's apartment. Gobie retailed his story all over the newspapers and television, adding new charges as he went along.

> **If you lie under scrutiny, you can no longer successfully refute anything, even the most outrageous story, because you have no credibility.**

But Frank did some important things right, and I admire him. He acted like a man with nothing to hide. He asked the House of Representatives' ethics committee to investigate his conduct. He admitted his mistakes with rueful humor. "I hadn't thought that gross stupidity was a violation of House rules," he said at the time.

When *The Advocate* asked Barney Frank almost 10 years later how he had survived the onslaught, he answered, "My defense was to tell the truth. I said I did a dumb thing, and people supported me because I leveled with them. People thought that I had done something wrong, but that it shouldn't end my political career."

That is exactly what happens when you tell the truth in the midst of a bad-news story. It is unpleasant. People probably won't like what you tell them. The truth will probably cost your brand some of its luster.

> **Telling the truth is often unpleasant. It will probably cost your brand some luster. But the higher your profile, the less likely you are to get away with anything but the truth.**

But that is not the point. The truth may be bitter medicine for a brand, but a lie is toxic. And the higher your profile, the less likely you are to get away with anything but the truth, since you will become a target for an army of ambitious reporters. Everyone will find out what you are trying to conceal anyway, so when in doubt, come clean.

BE PREPARED FOR THE DIME-DROPPERS

As I said earlier, if you are successful, it is a good bet that you have enemies in places you haven't even imagined. Somebody you fired eight years ago. Somebody whose girlfriend you stole in 1975. The bitter ex-husband you outgrew years earlier. Gadflies who think there is now money to be made in suing you. People who have disliked you from childhood. People you have not given a thought to for years.

One of the truly upsetting things about a bad-news story is the way it brings these enemies—known and unknown—out of the woodwork. They don't like you, they are reading negative things about you, and suddenly they have the means to get back at you. They have the power to keep the heat on.

Since the press is also interested in keeping a compelling story alive, reporters are generally eager to hear what these people have to say. Suddenly, a reporter is calling you and asking, "In college, were you really suspended for mooning the sorority house next door?" And if it's true, that becomes the next day's headline: "CEO Dropped Pants at ΧΕΓ Sorority."

Even worse than the questions the dime-droppers provoke from the responsible press are the unpleasant things that they spread unfiltered to less responsible outlets, such as Internet publications, gossip sheets, and chat rooms. And more upsetting than all three combined are the venomous anonymous letters that arrive at your door.

There is not much you can do about any of this nastiness, except steel yourself and your family for it. Again, by being forthright, you may contain a public airing of this stuff. Do not lie to the press about anything, no matter how old or embarrassing the story—

> **Bad-news stories bring dime-droppers out of the woodwork. So steel yourself and your family and do not lie about anything.**

even if it means that you are forever after known as the executive who dropped his trousers in 1983.

EVERY BRAND HAS INCENDIARY SPOTS; AVOID POURING GASOLINE ON YOURS

If you hope to finish a long and happy career without ever having become the central attraction in a media circus, it is very smart to be aware of the two types of stories that are most likely to open the big tent.

One is the "confirmation" story, in which you confirm suspicions about your brand, and the other is the "cross-cut" story, in which you prove that some key aspect of your brand is a lie.

Watergate is the perfect example of a confirmation story. Brand Nixon had always had its undertones of under-

> **The two types of stories that are most likely to provoke a media circus are the confirmation story and the cross-cut story. Avoid winding up in either one.**

handedness. Nixon had been called "Tricky Dick" ever since his 1950 Senate race. So when he was finally—finally!—caught red-handed orchestrating dirty tricks during the Watergate cover-up, the result was press pandemonium.

Remember, when your brand has a weakness of some sort, the kindling wood is always there underneath you. You have a choice. You can be very careful and allow it to disintegrate into compost over the years. Or you can strike a match to it, as Nixon did.

On the other hand, if a story cuts against the grain of your brand and is in conflict with what is generally believed about you, the press will jump on it with equal relish. This is the problem faced by televangelists Jimmy Swaggart and Jim Bakker. You preach about avoiding sin on TV, and then you are revealed to be a sinner yourself. Since few things are more fun for reporters than exposing hypocrites, press pandemonium ensues.

I don't know which is worse, the confirmation story or the cross-cut story. They are both very, very bad. Avoid sparking either one.

DON'T GO ON A JIHAD

It is a good bet that by the time the press is asking questions about how much you spend on your home furnishings or the way you treat salespeople, you are feeling pretty sorry for yourself. And, assuming that you are a prominent person who is used to being flattered all day long, you are probably feeling twice as sorry for yourself because criticism is so foreign to you.

It's crucial to remember that the world probably does not consider you deserving of pity. You are prominent, successful, lucky—and perceived as having done something wrong. You are probably not going to engender sympathy in a situation like this. And you will only seem more reprehensible if you appear angry at your critics or whine unbecomingly or try to shift the blame for your troubles to someone else.

Generally it is our own petards we are hoisted by—our own simple mistakes.

So don't blame your employees, your accountant, your plastic surgeon, your students, or your spouse. Former Trinity Law School dean Winston L. Frost offers an excellent example of how trying to shift blame can make a bad story worse. In 2001, Frost was accused of something unworthy of a seventh grader, let alone a law school dean: plagiarizing from the *Encyclopædia Britannica* in an article published in the school's law review.

Frost's response? He blamed it on the kids. He claimed that he had expected the law review's student staff to "fix" the missing footnotes in his piece, and they had failed to do so.

Instead of quieting the story, Frost's attempt to evade responsibility for his own work kept the story alive in the press and unleashed further allegations of plagiarism. It also raised serious questions about his fitness as an academic, as a teacher of the law, and as a major figure at a Christian university. And it did not save him from being fired.

Don't blame a vast, unnamed conspiracy. In late 2002, Senator Trent Lott was forced to resign his position as Senate Republican leader after a foolish remark praising Strom Thurmond's segregationist campaign for the presidency in 1948. Lott only made himself laughable afterwards by suggesting that he was a victim of discrimination. "There are some people in Washington who have been trying to nail me for a long time," he told the Associated Press. "When you're from Mississippi and you're a conservative and you're a Christian, there are a lot of people that don't like that. I fell into their trap and so I have only myself to blame."

Ranting about your enemies won't make you look like a martyr— but it will make you look like a baby, and possibly a dangerously paranoid baby.

The blame you lob at the press tends to boomerang. While a lot of people try to hold the media accountable for the bad press they or their organization is attracting, few have done so with the flair of Cardinal Bernard Law, the former Archbishop of Boston. In 1992, in the wake of

> It's important to remember that when you are the subject of negative press, you are not a sympathetic figure. So don't try to blame your troubles on
> - Anyone close to you
> - A conspiracy of unnamed enemies
> - The press itself

the *Boston Globe*'s coverage of the case of pedophile priest Reverend James R. Porter, Cardinal Law actually suggested that the *Globe* was so misguided that divine intervention was required: "By all means we call down God's power on the media, particularly the *Globe*."

Ultimately, however, God seemed to side with the *Globe* in this dispute. And the bitterness with which Law fought 10 years later to keep personnel documents about pedophile priests out of the *Globe*'s hands undermined his credibility as a potential reformer even as he was trying to paint himself as one—and contributed to the inevitability of his resigning.

Attacking the reporters who are tormenting you may make you feel better. But it generally does not convince the public that you are their victim. In fact, the public is usually delighted with the press for informing it of your shortcomings. Your attempts to shoot the messenger only seem like unwillingness to be held accountable for your own errors.

Finally, recognize that your perspective on your own troubles is likely to be warped. Don't try to be your own lawyer. Get advice from people who can be realistic about what is happening to you—not from people with a vested interest in helping you maintain your illusions.

> Don't try to be your own lawyer. Get advice from people who can be realistic about what is happening to you.

UPDATE YOUR EYEGLASS PRESCRIPTION REGULARLY

One of the toughest of all bad-news stories to bend your mind around and accept is the one that arises out of something you did that might have seemed perfectly fine a year earlier. The truth is, what is acceptable in one era is a disastrous affront in the next. Standards of behavior are constantly changing. It is very tricky to avoid tripping the wire that unleashes a press attack, because the wire moves all the time.

Even worse, the wire often moves abruptly higher overnight, after one particularly negative story awakens the press, the public, and the regulators to the possibility that standards have been set too low.

For example, the press generally ignored the infidelities of politicians until it encountered the strange case of presidential candidate Gary Hart in 1987. Hart offered a perverse challenge to reporters, answering questions about his womanizing by saying, "Follow me around. . . . If anybody wants to put a tail on me, go ahead. They'd be very bored." Well, the *Miami Herald* was following, and it was not bored. The *Herald* found Hart with a lovely young woman not his wife—Donna Rice. From then on, there was a new standard. If you were a politician and you were discovered to be unfaithful, the media no longer gave you a pass.

Business executives are now facing a similar watershed, albeit one that affects their professional, not their personal, lives. What is acceptable in the post-Enron world is very different from what was acceptable in the pre-Enron world. The lens that journalists, investors, employees, clients, and regulators apply to the activities of business executives has changed completely. And attitudes that would not have raised an eyebrow a few years ago now provoke outrage.

In 2003, Philip Purcell, CEO of Morgan Stanley, learned the hard way that a lack of contrition about any regulatory problem, big or small, will no longer fly. The day after prosecutors announced a $1.4 billion settlement with Wall Street firms for abuses during the high-tech stock boom—including $125 million from Morgan Stanley—Purcell said publicly, "I don't see anything in the settlement that will concern the retail investor about Morgan Stanley."

Reaction from New York State Attorney General Eliot Spitzer and SEC Chairman William Donaldson was swift and severe. Not only did they take the opportunity to remind the public of problematic things in Morgan Stanley's record, but Donaldson also pointed to Purcell's "disturbing and misguided perspective on Morgan Stanley's alleged misconduct." Needless to say, none of this added luster to Brand Purcell.

It is pointless to fight against a new standard of behavior. Instead, try to adjust to the times and see your behavior in a new light. And if you attract a negative story because you have not adjusted quickly enough, apologize. Purcell, who is a very capable executive, corrected his mistake quickly.

> **Don't try to fight changing standards. Recognize that what was acceptable yesterday may cause you a world of trouble today.**

Clearly, the heightened press scrutiny that business executives are now subject to is a direct result of the corporate scandals and high-tech stock crash of the early 2000s. I am sure that a lot of executives secretly hope that once the stock market turns up again, the attention will fade and standards will loosen.

Again, the Gary Hart story is instructive. That story took off because of the peculiar dare that Hart made, but it provoked a new level of scrutiny that every politician has been subject to ever since.

It is important to understand that people are interested in the news for the same reason that many people watch NASCAR racing: They are hoping to see a car crash into a wall and go up in flames. Once they comprehend that your particular world offers the potential for a crash as spectacular as that of Enron, they are not going to turn away again. The scrutiny becomes a fact of life. Standards rise.

Of course, if the standards of behavior in your world now seem too high for you, you do have one option: Try a new profession. As a business executive, you cannot get drunk in public and get into a bar fight without inviting the outraged attention of the press. As a pro athlete? The world can barely conceal its collective yawn.

DO NOT LET THEM SEE YOU SWEAT

The fact is, when you are in the middle of a bad-news story, you are thrust into an unknown world, one where you no longer have control over your daily activities because you are taking "incoming" all the time. So don't be surprised if the experience leads to self-doubt or the desire not to go on.

However, it's a mistake to give up just because you are tired of the heat. I learned years ago that if you don't let them see you sweat, you generally don't sweat all that long.

Hewlett-Packard CEO Carly Fiorina is a prime example of what steadiness in the face of bad press can do for your brand. When both the Hewlett and the Packard families came out in 2001 in opposition to the merger she was engineering between Hewlett-Packard and Compaq, Fiorina's personal brand took a number of serious hits.

Her critics suggested that she was a slick operator who was out to destroy the celebrated H-P culture for her own financial gain. The dime-droppers came out of the woodwork, and the press printed plenty of rumors about Marie Antoinette–like behavior. "Some of the things said about Ms. Fiorina are the Silicon Valley equivalent of urban legends," reported the *New York Times*. "One is that she always travels with an entourage, including a hairdresser. No, say friends and colleagues, she has her hair cut at a place in a Stanford shopping center."

A proxy fight over the merger followed, and then accusations that she had cheated to win the proxy vote. Throughout the onslaught, Fiorina demonstrated a calm, unshakable conviction that she was making the right decision for her organization.

If she had retreated under pressure and given up the idea of the merger, it would have confirmed that she was what her critics charged: all spin and no substance. Instead, she convinced a lot of skeptics that she was the right leader for H-P. In his book *Backfire*, Peter Burrows describes the transformation of Brand Fiorina after the proxy fight wound up in court:

> Her rock-solid testimony gained her new admirers. She'd won by being credible and through understanding her business. Fiorina, the ultimate marketer, left the trial with a new reputation intact: that of a CEO who could speak credibly about the business and move past a proxy battle to get the job done.

The terrific job that Fiorina subsequently did of integrating the two companies only cemented this reputation.

People will take your measure in a crisis. As painful as public criticism can be, it gives you a rare opportunity to prove how resilient you are. If you are able to handle a harsh spotlight coolly, you may wind up like Fiorina. You may wind up advancing your brand in the midst of an attack in a way that you could not have advanced it if life had been a little easier on you.

> **If you handle it well, bad press will give you a chance to prove how resilient you are and may eventually wind up enhancing your brand.**

Though it may not feel like it when the antiaircraft guns are firing at you, good things really can come out of bad press. So, stay calm and keep flying the plane.

EVERYBODY COULDA BEEN A CONTENDER; MAKE SURE YOU STAY ONE

The movie *About Schmidt*, for which Jack Nicholson won the 2003 Golden Globe award for Best Actor in a Drama, opens with a terrible scene: the typical retirement party where coworkers sum up the career of the retiree.

The young guy who is taking over for the Nicholson character stands up and tries to say a few words about him. It's like a living eulogy, only everyone is eating chicken in a banquet hall instead of clutching a handkerchief in a funeral parlor. Unfortunately, all the guy can come up with is the hollow cliché that Nicholson has left "big shoes" for him to fill, and the whole room senses that he is having to struggle even to say that much.

Here is the point: Nicholson has put in 40 years at an insurance company, and his colleagues have almost nothing to say about him. The scene is awful only because it's so real. Every day tens of thousands of people retire, and their coworkers find it hard to make the most cursory remarks about them.

Yet I would bet that if you had asked those same faceless people at age 20 or 25 what they would want said at their retirement party, it would be far different from an empty "He will be missed." Most 25-year-olds would say they would want to be remembered this way: "Incredibly innovative and creative, took bold risks, sensitive person, fantastic manager, great leader."

The sorry fact is that somewhere between ages 25 and 65, most ambitious people go wrong. They start their careers ready to set the world on fire, yet at some point they make decisions that give them a personal brand that is notable only for its mediocrity.

Unfortunately, even if you follow every rule in this book, middle age and mid-career are dangerous. Your responsibilities are growing. You may have children. Your parents are aging. Your significant other's parents are aging. You probably have a mortgage. All these things conspire against risk and change. So it's easy to simply stop moving forward, become another cog in the wheel, and wind up with a reputation that spells "going nowhere."

> Even if you follow every rule in the book, middle age and mid-career are dangerous for your brand.

How do you avoid the bitterness of looking back and thinking of what you could have been, instead of the nonentity you have become? Here are ten suggestions to help you keep the momentum going long after your colleagues' brands have settled into middle-aged inertia.

1. DON'T BE A GENERIC, BE TYLENOL

You can either be generic acetaminophen or be Tylenol. The active ingredient is the same, but Tylenol is a cult. When there is a crisis—the baby's got a fever!—most people choose Tylenol.

Generic acetaminophen may be just as effective and a lot cheaper, but it has no cult.

Don't allow fear and sluggishness to turn you from the Tylenol you once were into a generic in middle age. Don't be afraid to part ways with your more generic peers. Your brand is constantly being compared with theirs, and the only way to win brand loyalty from your bosses is to offer something distinctive.

> **Your brand is constantly being compared with your peers'. Don't be afraid to offer something distinctive.**

2. GET BACK ON THE HORSE

As I've said before, the organizational pyramid narrows as it rises, and the higher you get within an organization, the fewer opportunities there are for you to move up.

So the chances are good that no matter how terrific you are, you may be passed over for a promotion that you feel you should have gotten. Unfortunately, a lot of people become discouraged very, very easily. They think, "I didn't get the promotion I wanted, so I no longer care about my career. I'm just here to punch it."

It's foolish to throw in the towel because of a setback or two. For example, Jerry Levin, the former CEO of AOL Time Warner, was passed over for the job of president of Time Inc. in 1986 and almost quit when the job went instead to his long-time rival Nick Nicholas. That would have been a mistake, because six years later, the tables turned. Nicholas was forced out, and Levin became CEO of Time Warner.

If you are passed over for a promotion, make it clear to your bosses that you do not by any means count yourself out of the game. How do you do that? Well . . .

> **It's foolish to throw in the towel because of a setback or two.**

3. IT NEVER HURTS TO ASK

Many people are not interested in getting ahead, but only in getting by. So stand out from the crowd by asking your bosses for more.

> Ask for opportunities and promotions. It will remind your bosses that you are someone to keep in mind for big jobs.

Say, "Why am I not being promoted? What can I do to earn a new opportunity? Can I take on some new responsibilities?"

If you show your bosses that you think of yourself someone who should be progressing, they are likely to look at you in the same way.

4. NEVER SELL YOUR BRAND FOR SHORT MONEY

There is a great scene in the classic 1954 movie *On the Waterfront* in which the washed-up boxer played by Marlon Brando reproaches his brother for convincing him to throw a prizefight in exchange for next to nothing. "I coulda been a contender," Brando says, painfully.

Well, a lot of people in business, too, coulda been contenders, if they hadn't sold their brands rather cheaply.

Two investment professionals I know offer the perfect example. A few years ago, they told me that they were being offered jobs in operations away from the headquarters of their organization. I gave them some advice: "Say that you'll take the job for 18 months, but that you don't want a raise."

They found this idea very curious. "Why wouldn't we want a raise?" they asked.

"Because," I told them, "if you take the raise, you'll have been bought. If you don't take the raise, they will feel obligated to bring you back to headquarters with the experience you've gained—and you will be in line for bigger jobs."

Instead, they both insisted on raises, they both were kept out in the field too long, and they both got passed over for promotions.

Once people figure out that they can buy you for 5 or 10 percent of your salary, you've entered the world's oldest profession—and I don't mean banking. They no longer have to give you interesting opportunities in order to keep you. They no longer have to offer you a dynamic career trajectory. They just have to throw a few trinkets your way.

Do not allow your bosses to think of you as easily bought. Never put yourself out of the running for bigger jobs in exchange for a small amount of money. Of course it's tough to turn down any amount of money when you have a lot of personal responsibilities—but think of it as an investment in your career. When you finally arrive at the top of the pyramid, the amount you gain will make the amount you have given up to get there look like a pittance.

> Do not allow your bosses to think of you as easily bought.

5. IF LIGHTNING IS ABOUT TO STRIKE, MAKE SURE YOU ARE STANDING IN AN OPEN FIELD

In your career, you often cannot make change happen. It will happen around you. You won't control the moment when you are plucked from the crowd and given an opportunity that is orders of magnitude greater than those your peers will be given. Instead, the moment will control you.

Sometimes events will take well-deserved opportunities away from you. You may be a fantastic marketing person, but if your organization is having an operational crisis and there appear to be some shenanigans with the books, you will probably not get the CEO's job at that point. Instead, an operations person will win. That is the reputation that is needed at the time.

And sometimes events will throw surprising opportunities your way. For example, Andy Lack, who became chairman of Sony's music division in 2003, has had a career that has included more than one unexpected leap because he offered the right brand at the right time. As a CBS television producer in 1993 with a background in both advertising and theater, he was recommended by Tom Brokaw for a job as an executive producer at *NBC Nightly News*. Instead, he wound up getting the much bigger job of president of NBC News. With its news division reeling from a scandal and losing money, NBC was attracted to Lack's reputation as someone who could bring the panache of entertainment to news programs.

Ten years later, Lack surprised the world again. He was tapped to head Sony Music when his experience in the music business was precisely zero. But Sony Music was losing money and flailing in the face of Internet piracy. In other words, it was ready for an outsider, and Lack was an outsider with experience in turning around a media property. Again, the right reputation at the right moment.

You probably are not going to be able to engineer the historic moment that will favor your particular brand. Bosses tend to frown upon the organizational equivalent of the firefighter who commits arson in order to become a hero. So what can you do?

You can be in position in case the fates do align in your direction.

> **Often, you cannot control the events that will lead to a promotion. But you can make sure that you are in position to be the obvious choice.**

Make sure you plant yourself where you are most likely to be needed, because that is where the opportunities are. For example, if your organization is headed by a pair of executives in their late fifties or early sixties and you hope to succeed them, do not accept a transfer to Singapore. The people in front of you may decide to retire any day, and you will be out of position. Your brand will be forgotten, and someone who works for you now will probably be your boss by the time you get back.

Be ready for opportunities in unexpected places—but while you are traveling down the highway, be careful not to take a turn-off onto a dead-end road.

6. GAMBLE SHREWDLY

There are moments when you simply have to bet your brand in order to move ahead. For example, let's say you are working for a large nation-wide charity, and the number one thing it needs is someone who can figure out how to raise funds for a handful of local organizations that are doing a terrible job.

It is apparent to everyone that turning things around at these organizations will not be easy. But if you decide to take that job and you are successful at it, your reputation will be that of someone who stepped up when other people didn't have the courage, was loyal to the organization, and actually accomplished what the organization required most.

That's a real feather for your brand. One advantage I always thought I had over a lot of very, very smart people with whom I was competing was that I was goal-oriented— goal-oriented in terms of what the organization and my bosses needed most, not what I needed. I understood what the business required, and I made it happen.

> There are times when you have to bet your brand in order to move ahead. Promising to accomplish something difficult is a risk, but one that is well worth taking.

Whenever you promise to accomplish something difficult, you are taking a risk—but it's a risk that is probably well worth taking. However, they do not call them risks for nothing. Any time you say you will do something major, you have to be prepared to fall on your sword and leave the organization if you fail to do it.

Fortunately, the people at the next organization for which you are interested in working probably won't know how unsuccessful you were. If the audience is fresh, your brand will be untarnished.

Unfortunately, when you are in mid-career, you cannot change organizations as lightly as you could earlier. When you are in your twenties or thirties, if you have three jobs in five years, anyone considering hiring you thinks, "It's experience." When you are in your forties or fifties, if you have three jobs in five years, people assume that there is something wrong with you. Your brand becomes tainted.

7. CREATE A BRAIN TRUST

To get ahead in mid-career, you have to take risks, but you can't afford to have too many risks turn out badly. So how do you make sure that you always bet your brand wisely?

> **Develop a circle of people whose advice you trust to help you bet wisely.**

One of the best of all ways is by developing over time a small circle of people you can talk to whose advice you can trust. Hopefully, these people are politically savvy and organizationally savvy, the type of people who keep their ear to the ground and know how to interpret the things they hear.

Unfortunately, once they have any kind of power, a lot of people say, "I can make decisions by myself. I don't take advice from other people." That is simply dumb.

8. TINKER WITH SUCCESS

Recently, John Hancock brought in an outsider for a high-ranking position within the company. After he had been with us for a month, he was telling me cautiously about the people he had met and what he had seen.

When we were through talking about his impressions, I asked him a question: "So what exactly are you hearing about my reputation among the senior people?" I added, "I'm an adult. Let's not sugar-coat this thing."

"Well," he said, "some of them truly fear you because they know you don't suffer fools gladly." He added, "I haven't heard anybody say yet that you are unfair. And it's clear that telling the truth is very important. But there is some palpable fear."

My initial reaction to that was, "So what?" But when I thought about it afterwards, I thought, "How much fear is enough? How much fear is too much? Why am I sending off that vibe?"

I was doing it partially because a skittish economy had put the life insurance industry under a lot of pressure, and I wanted my senior people to know that a lot was at stake. And I was doing it partially because I wasn't taking enough vacation time, and I was not doing the tough things the moment demanded in the kindest and gentlest manner.

The problem with putting too much fear into your brand is that you won't get enough truth in return. So I decided I had to dial it down a bit.

The fact is that you are never too old to adjust your brand—and never too powerful. Unfortunately, a lot of people with power say, "I'm here now. I'm in charge. I never have to justify my behavior again."

That seems to be the sentiment George W. Bush was expressing to Bob Woodward in Woodward's 2002 best-seller *Bush at War*. Bush told Woodward that he was deliberately provocative with his war cabinet in order to push them to make decisions about Afghanistan. When Woodward asked if Bush had explained to them that he was planning on testing them that way, Bush said something revealing in response:

> I do not need to explain why I say things. That's the interesting thing about being the President. Maybe somebody needs to explain to me why they say something, but I don't feel like I owe anybody an explanation.

I would beg to differ. You never reach a point where you are done justifying yourself—not if you hope to be reelected, not if you hope to win the Nobel Peace Prize, not if you hope to be lauded by the history books. You are building your reputation until you die. And even the best reputations take some unexpected turns.

For example, when Jack Welch retired from General Electric in 2001 crowned with laurel leaves, I am sure that the last thing he expected was to have his golden reputation dented by a messy divorce. Yet in court filings a year later, his wife Jane Welch made public the degree to which GE shareholders were subsidizing a lifestyle that he could easily have afforded to maintain on his own.

Welch was rich, he was retired, he had signed a contract giving him those perks, and he could have just ignored the blow to his brand. But the truth is, the richer and more powerful you become, the more likely you are to want one of the few things that cannot be bought—to be remembered well.

"So here's my dilemma," Welch wrote in a *Wall Street Journal* op-ed. "Do I keep the contract and look like someone who's out of touch in today's post-Enron world? Or do I modify a legal contract and take the hit of being perceived as having done something improper?"

He wound up deciding to modify the contract, giving up over $2 million a year in perks. Clearly, he had weighed the options and decided it was better to be seen as someone who had corrected an impropriety than to seem arrogantly out of touch with the times.

Welch is a very smart guy. There are very few consumer product brands that survive for 40 years without adjustments. Don't expect that your personal brand will survive without adjustments, either.

> You are building your brand until the day you die, so expect to make adjustments.

9. DO NOT CROSS THE LINES OF INTEGRITY

We have already talked about avoiding the pitfalls of arrogance. Enough said. Do not lie, cheat, or steal. Whatever power you have amassed by mid-career, it is not enough to protect you from disgrace.

> Don't lie, cheat, or steal. Power won't protect you from disgrace.

10. UNDERSTAND THAT THE UNEXAMINED REPUTATION IS NOT WORTH HAVING

If I could condense all the advice in this book into just one line, that line would have to be this: "Be conscious every day of what you are building."

That alone will set you apart from 99 percent of the people you will meet in organizational life, all of whom are too busy worrying "What about me?" to consider the character they are assembling in other people's eyes.

Every day of your working life, you are selling yourself through the things you do, the words you choose, the way you treat people, and the way you look. But you are not just making an argument for yourself— you are also engaged in an act of self-creation. You are constructing the

person who will someday be thought of and remembered as a supreme-
ly successful human being—or not.

Always try to be aware of what you are creating, and try not to fool
yourself. Intending to be a force for innovation, a risk taker, a sensitive
person, a fantastic manager, and a great leader will not make you one.
If that is the personal brand you want, you have to prove to the world
that you possess all those great qualities.

You have to use that brand as a template for all your actions.
Ultimately, if your brand is to mean anything, you have to live it, and
you have to go on living it to the very end.

INDEX